# Dreamweaver®

## MX 2004

A c c e l e r a t e d

YJ IT Publishing Team

Manager: **Suzie Lee**
Chief Editor: **Angelica Lim**
Developmental Editor: **Colleen Wheeler Strand**
Production Editor: **Patrick Cunningham**
Technical Editor: **Katrine Poon**
Editors: **Carol Loh, Peter Turner, Sas Jacobs**
Proofreader: **Semtle**
Cover Designer: **Changwook Lee**
Book Designer: **Semtle**
Production Control: **Ann Lee**
Indexer: **Katrine Poon**

ISBN: 89-314-3507-X

Printed and bound in the Republic of Korea.

**How to contact us**

E-mail: support@youngjin.com
        feedback@youngjin.com.sg
Address: YoungJin.com
1623-10, Seocho-dong, Seocho-gu, Seoul 137-878, Korea
Telephone: +65-6327-1161
Fax: +65-6327-1151

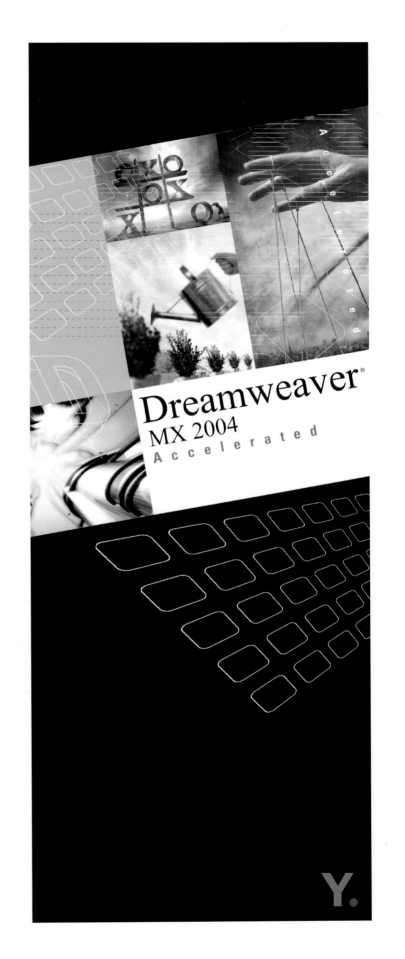

Dreamweaver® MX 2004 Accelerated

contents

# Installing Dreamweaver MX 2004 › › ›

*This section provides information about installing and using Dreamweaver MX 2004. Instructions for downloading and installing Macromedia's 30-day trial version of Dreamweaver MX 2004 are also included.*

## Downloading a Trial Version

If you do not have a copy of Dreamweaver MX 2004, you can download a 30-day trial copy from the Macromedia Web site.

[1] Start Internet Explorer. Type in http://www.macromedia.com in the address field and hit [Enter]. From the menu at the top of the Web page, choose [Downloads] - [Free Trials].

[2] Find Dreamweaver MX 2004 in the product list and click on [Try].

<< tip

### If You Do Not Have a Password

If you don't have a Macromedia password, select [No, I will create one now.] and then click [Continue]. Type in the relevant information on the password setup page and then click [Continue].

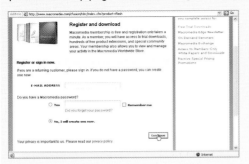

[3] In the Register and download window, type in your e-mail address and your Macromedia password (if you have one) and click [Continue].

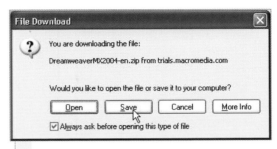

**4** On the Macromedia Trial Downloads page, you can download the trial program in the language and the operating system of your choice. In the Dreamweaver MX 2004 drop-down menu, choose English | Windows | 62.87MB.

**5** After selecting the system requirements for Dreamwearver MX 2004 and Dreamwearver MX Professional 2004, click on [Download]. When the File Download dialog box appears, click [Save].

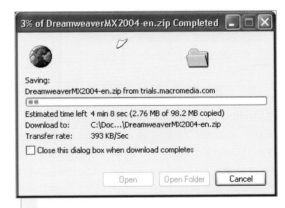

**6** In the Save As dialog box, choose the folder where you wish to save the trial program and then click [Save].

**7** Your download will begin automatically. Extract the file after downloading.

## Installing Dreamweaver MX 2004

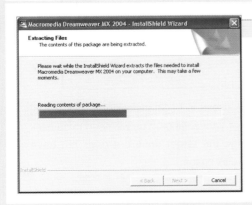

**1** Double-click the Dreamweaver MX 2004 Installer.exe file to start the installation. You should see the dialog box pictured on the left.

2 When you see the above dialog box, click [Next] to continue.

3 Before you can install the file, you will be asked to accept the license agreement. Click the [Yes] button to accept the agreement and carry on with the installation. If you click [No], the installation will end.

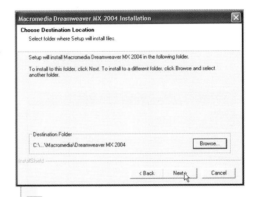

4 In this step, you will decide where to install the program. Click [Next] to install Dreamweaver in the Programs folder, or use the [Browse] button to choose a different location.

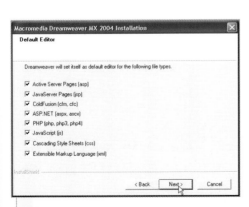

5 You will then be asked which file types you want to associate with Dreamweaver.

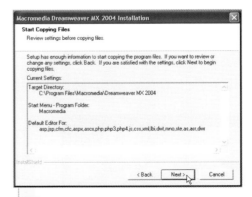

6 Click [Next] to begin installing or click [Back] to change your settings. You will need to go back to change the target drive if it does not have enough disk space.

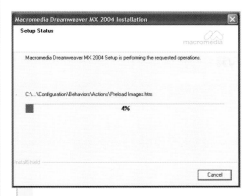

7 Once you've clicked [Next] the installation will begin.

8 When the installation has finished, you will see a message stating that the installation is complete. Click the [Finish] button to close the dialog box.

<< tip

### Installing in Microsoft Windows 98 or 2000

When installing Dreamweaver MX 2004 on Windows 98 or 2000, you will see a message that tells you to restart your computer after the installation is complete. Click [Finish] to end the installation and reboot your computer. You must reboot the computer in order for Dreamweaver to work properly.

## Downloading Extensions

1 Go to Macromedia's Web site (www.macromedia.com). Select [Downloads] - [Free Trials] from the menu bar.

2 On the Downloads page, look under All Product Downloads and click the Extensions link next to Dreamweaver MX 2004.

3 You will see the Dreamweaver Exchange page. Click on the Search Exchanges button on the right of the Web page. When the Exchange Search page appears, enter the desired extension name and click the Search button. Click the Download button in the extension's Availability field.

4 You will be asked to sign in. Fill in your email address and password and follow the instructions to download the extension to your computer.

Chapter | 1

# Dreamweaver MX 2004 - The Basics

Welcome to Dreamweaver MX 2004! Dreamweaver is a powerful Web page creation program created by Macromedia. It's included in the Macromedia Studio MX 2004 software bundle. It's important to learn the basics and build up your skills before you start working with the more advanced features within Dreamweaver MX 2004. In this chapter, you will be introduced to some of the basic features that you'll need to be familiar with before you can start creating Web pages.

# About Dreamweaver

S ince its introduction, Dreamweaver has become one of the most popular Web page design programs in the world. It can be used to create and maintain an entire Web site, and is flexible enough to be used by both Web designers and programmers. In this section, you will learn about the top features in Dreamweaver, the Dreamweaver interface, and how to set up a Web site.

## Key Features

### Templates

It's easy to start creating Web pages in Dreamweaver because you can choose from a number of Dreamweaver's predefined templates. You can also create your own templates. When building a Web site with many pages, templates save you time by letting you create new Web pages while maintaining a uniform look.

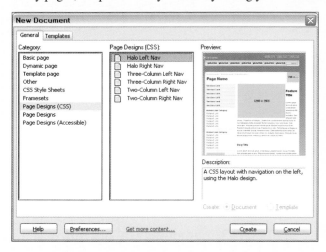

Using Templates to Create a New Web Page

### Document Views in Dreamweaver

Dreamweaver is versatile in that it supports three different views for different folks who work with Web pages: Design View, Code View, and Split View. The Design View, which is for designers and those who prefer a visual interface, shows the Web page as it will appear within a Web browser. The Code View, which is for programmers and those who are comfortable working with code, shows the HTML code for the Web page. The Split View is probably the best view to work in because it shows both the Web page and the HTML code.

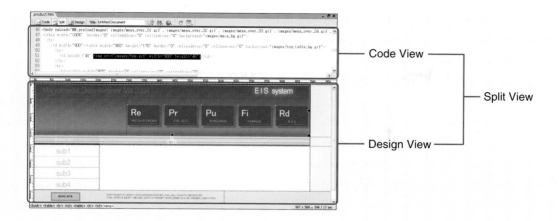

Code View

Split View

Design View

## Enhanced Support for Cascading Style Sheets

Dreamweaver lets you save a set of commonly used formatting styles, such as a specific font color and size, and apply these styles at one go on multiple Web pages. These styles are saved as Cascading Style Sheets. Dreamweaver contains a CSS Styles panel and a CSS style rule inspector (new in Dreamweaver MX 2004) to help you work with Cascading Style Sheets. The CSS Styles panel shows styles and their settings while the CSS style rule inspector (or CSS properties panel) allows you to make detailed modifications to CSS styles.

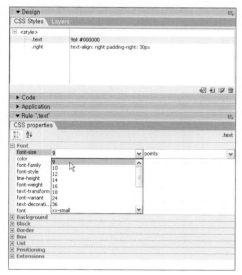

You can also work with Cascading Style Sheets using the Style drop-down box in the Properties Inspector.

You can also use Dreamweaver MX 2004 to easily insert styles into a Web page. Select [Modify] - [Page Properties] to bring up the Page Properties dialog box. This will allow you to edit page attributes such as the font face and link styles, and automatically create appropriate styles.

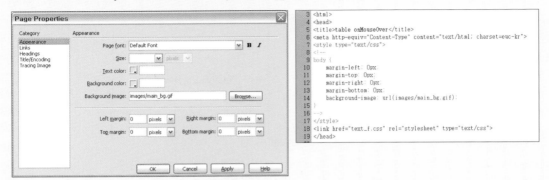

## Dreamweaver and Fireworks MX 2004

Dreamweaver MX 2004 allows you to edit images using Fireworks, a graphics editing program also made by Macromedia. When an image is selected, a Fireworks icon appears in the Properties Inspector. Click the [Edit] icon (⬛) to open and edit the image using Fireworks.

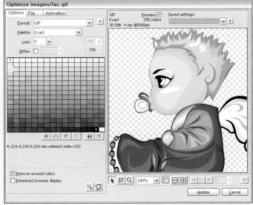

## Browser Testing

It is important to test each Web page in different Web browsers to make sure your pages display correctly. A browser compatibility test is automatically run when a Dreamweaver document is created. Dreamweaver uses the default browser to check that the page doesn't contain unsupported tags or other features. Unsupported features will appear underlined in red in Code view.

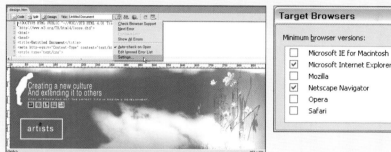

```
',`images/images/menu_over_02.gif`,`images/images/menu_over_03.gif`,`images/images/menu_over_04.gif`,`imag
x: width:125px; height:113px; z-index:1">
">

Over="MM_swapImage('Image2','','images/images/menu_over_01.gif',1)"><img src="images/images/menu_up_01.gif

Over="MM_swapImage('Image3','','images/images/menu_over_02.gif',1)"><img src="images/images/menu_up_02.gif
```

## FTP Security

Dreamweaver MX 2004 includes FTP functionality so there is no need to use an external FTP program. Secure FTP encrypts all transferred files and can prevent unauthorized persons from seeing the files or FTP settings.

## Server Behaviors

Dreamweaver is suitable for both Web designers and programmers. The features within Dreamweaver allow both groups to create Web applications. Dreamweaver supports server languages such as Cold Fusion, ASP, PHP, and JSP and allows easy connection to a database.

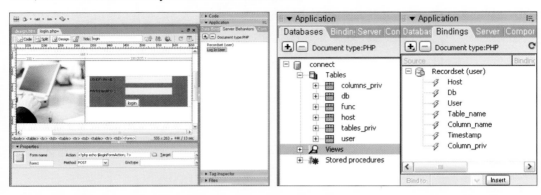

## Management of Assets

The library stores assets that are used in a site, allowing you to use them over and over again as needed.

## Working with Microsoft Word and Excel

Content from Microsoft Word and Excel documents can be copied and pasted into Dreamweaver MX 2004. When pasted, font and color settings from the original documents are included within Dreamweaver.

# The Dreamweaver Interface

If you haven't used earlier versions of Dreamweaver, the interface can look a little complicated at first. In this section, we will look closely at the different elements that make up the Dreamweaver interface.

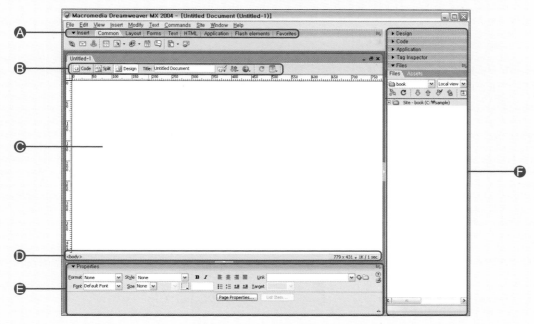

**Ⓐ** **Insert Bar**

**Ⓑ** **Document Toolbar**

**Ⓒ** **Document Window**

**Ⓓ** **Tag Selector and the Status Bar**

**Ⓔ** **Properties Inspector**

**Ⓕ** **Panel Groups**

## Ⓐ Insert Bar

The Insert bar contains buttons in categories such as [Common], [Text], [Layers], and [HTML]. You can choose a different category from the drop-down menu on the left side of the Insert bar. When you point at a button, a brief explanation appears. Some buttons support pop-up menus. When you select an option from a pop-up it becomes the default button. Let's have a look at the different categories.

**a. Common**: The Common category contains buttons for inserting common objects, such as links, images, and tables.

**b. Layout**: The Layout category is used to insert tables, div tags, layers, and frames. When working with tables, you can select from three different modes: Standard (default), Expanded, and Layout.

**c. Forms**: The Forms category includes buttons for working with forms and form elements.

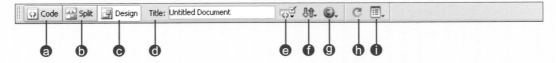

**d. Text**: The Text category is used to insert HTML tags that relate to text, such as formatting, paragraph, list, and heading tags.

**e. HTML**: The HTML category is used to insert horizontal lines, meta information, tables, frames, and scripts.

**f. Application**: The Application category relates to pages that contain programming languages, such as ASP, ASP.NET, ColdFusion, JSP, and PHP. There are buttons to insert programming code for recordsets; dynamic form elements; and inserting, updating, and deleting records.

**g. Flash elements**: The Flash elements category is used to work with Flash images.

**h. Favorites**: The Favorites category can be customized so that it contains commonly-used buttons.

Right-click to customize your favorite objects.

**B Document Toolbar**

The Document Toolbar allows you to change the way you view your document, and to make other changes, such as changing your page's title.

**a. Show Code View**: Shows the HTML code for the page in the Document window.

**b. Show Split View**: Displays both the HTML code and the page design in the Document window.

**c. Show Design View**: Displays the page design in the Document window.

**d. Title**: Shows the document title.

**e. No Browser/Check Errors**: Checks compatibility between Web browsers.

**f. File Management**: Brings up the File Management pop-up menu.

**g. Preview/Debug in Browser**: Opens the document to preview it in a Web browser. You can select the browser from the menu or press [F12] to use the default browser.

**h. Refresh Design View**: Shows any modifications made in Code View in Design View.

**i. View Options**: Used to set visual, grid, and ruler options within the Document window.

<< tip

## View Shortcuts

The shortcut keys for switching between Code View and Design View are [Ctrl]-[~] for PCs or [Command]-[ ´ ] for Macintosh computers. When Split View is shown, the shortcut keys change the focus between panes.

### ◉ Document Window

The Document window is where you will design a Web page. The Document window can be displayed in Design View, Code View, or Split View. This is covered in detail on page 12.

### ◉ Tag Selector and the Status Bar

*Tag Selector*: The Tag Selector shows the HTML tags around the current item. Click a tag to select it and its contents. If you click the <body> tag, you can select all the contents in the document.

*Window Size Pop-Up Menu*: Use this pop-up menu to set the Document window to a predetermined size. You can also define your own size settings.

*Document Size and Estimated Download Time*: The right-hand side of the [Window Size] pop-up menu shows the document size and estimated download time. This includes all files within the page, such as images and other media.

### ◉ Properties Inspector

The Properties Inspector displays the properties for the page element that is currently selected. The properties displayed in the Properties Inspector will differ depending on the element selected (e.g., text, image, layer, frame, or Flash element). By default, the Properties Inspector appears at the bottom of the work area, but it can be dragged to any location on the screen. Click ( ▦ ), at the top-left of the Properties Inspector and drag the window to its new location.

You can hide and show the Properties Inspector by selecting [Windows] - [Properties] or by using the [Ctrl]-[F3] shortcut keys.

The properties of the current page can be viewed by clicking the [Page Properties] button ( Page Properties... ).

**Ⓕ Panel Groups**

There are many panels in Dreamweaver, and panels with related functions are grouped together in a panel group. For example, the Design panel group contains the CSS Styles panel and the Layers panel. When Dreamweaver starts up, the panel groups are not expanded and you won't be able to see the individual panels. Let's learn to expand panel groups and hide panels.

• Expanding or Contracting Panel Groups

Click on the [Expand/Contract] triangle (  ) on the left side of the panel group title bar.

• Displaying or Hiding Panels

To display a panel group, select the [Windows] menu from the main menu and click on the name of the panel group. Panel groups that are currently visible will show a checkmark. To hide a panel group, uncheck the panel group's name in the menu.

<< tip

**Panel Shortcuts**

If you are having trouble finding a panel, you can organize all the panels by selecting [Window] - [Arrange panels]. You can hide all panels by using the [F4] key. Hidden panels can be displayed by pressing [F4] again.

# Setting Up Your Web Site

Depending on the type of Web site you are working on, a Dreamweaver site can consist of up to 3 different folders, namely the local folder (also know as the local site), the remote folder (or the remote site), and the testing server folder.

## Setting Up a Local Site

The local site can be a folder on your machine or on a network server. It is where you store all the files you are working on for the Web site. These could include text documents, images, Flash files, JavaScript files, and CSS files. When you change a file name, Dreamweaver will automatically update all other files on the local site that refer to that file. This is especially important if your Web site is very complex and has numerous interlinks.

You can define the local site in either the Basic or Advanced mode. The basic approach uses a setup wizard to help you define a local site. All you need to do is answer a few questions. If this is your first time building a Web site, you may find the basic approach less intimidating. But I would recommend that you use the advanced approach because it gives you more options.

### Using the Basic Approach

Let's learn to set up a local site using the basic approach.

1. On the startup screen, click on the [Dreamweaver Site...] option under the Create New menu. This launches the Site Definition dialog box.

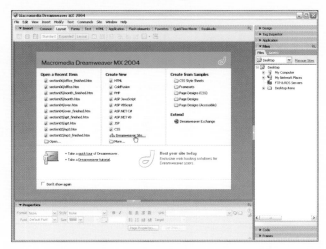

2. Select the [Basic] tab to bring up the first screen of the Site Definition Wizard. Type in a name for your Web site and click [Next].

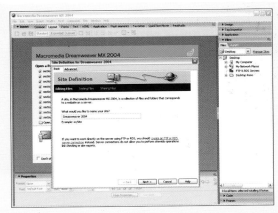

3. The next screen appears, asking if you wish to work with a server technology. Select [No] if you are working on a static Web site with no dynamic pages. (A dynamic Web page is one that lets you send or retrieve information from the Web server.) Examples include a log-in page, a search engine, or a shopping cart. Let's keep it simple for now and click [Next].

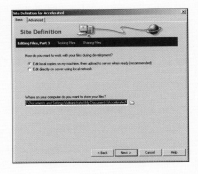

4. The next screen appears, asking how you wish to work with your Web page. Choose the recommended option–editing local copies on your machine, and then uploading them when ready.

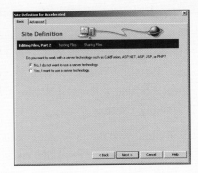

5. Click on the folder icon ( ) to specify the local folder where you want to store your Web site files. The Choose Local Root Folder for Site dialog box appears. Navigate to a folder in the dialog box. Alternatively, you can click on the [New Folder] icon ( ) to create a new folder. Click [Open]. Then click [Select]. The dialog box closes. Click [Next] to continue.

6. The next screen appears, asking how you want to connect with your server. Select [None] from the drop-down menu. You can define your connection later. Click [Next].

7. The next screen appears, showing a summary of the settings you have specified. Click [Done].

8. In the Files panel, you will see the root folder of your new Web site. You will also see all the files in the root folder, if you have any. You are now ready to start adding Web pages, folders, and images to your Web site.

## Using the Advanced Approach

Another way of setting up a local site is to use the advanced approach. Let's learn to do this.

1. On the startup screen, click the [Dreamweaver Site...] option. When the Site Definition dialog box appears, click on the [Advanced] tab.

2. Check that the Local Info option under Category is selected. On the right of the Category menu, you will see the options available for the Local Info category. Type in a name for your Web site in the Site Name field. Click on the folder icon () next to the Local Root Folder field to specify the local folder where you want to store your Web site files.

3. The Choose Local Root Folder for Site dialog box pops up. Navigate to a folder in the dialog box. Alternatively, you can click on the [New Folder] icon () to create a new folder. Click [Open] and then click [Select]. The dialog box closes. Click [Next] to continue.

4. Click on the folder icon () next to the Default Images Folder field to create or select a default folder for storing images for your Web site. Make sure that you choose a folder inside the local root folder.

5. Type in the URL (Web address) of your Web site. Click [OK].

6. In the Files panel, you will see the root folder of your new Web site. You will also see all the files in the root folder, if you have any. You are now ready to start adding Web pages, folders, and images to your Web site.

# Setting Up a Remote Site

A remote site is a directory on a Web server that is hosting your Web site. To make your Web site accessible on the Internet, you need to set up a remote site. You then need to upload your Web site to the Web server through a process known as File Transfer Protocol, or FTP. This section describes how you can set up and connect to a remote site, as well as upload and download files from a remote site.

1. Open the Site Definition dialog box. As shown in the preceding pages, you can do this by either selecting [Dreamweaver Site...] - [Advanced] from the startup screen, or by selecting [Site Menu] - [Manage Sites] - [Edit] from the Files panel.

2. Click on the Remote Info option under Category. Select FTP from the Access drop-down menu. Next, type in the address of the Web server (in the FTP Host field), your site's directory path on the Web server (in the Host Directory field), your login name, and your password.

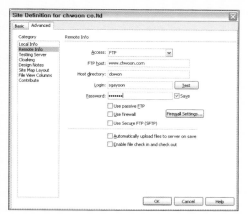

&lt;&lt; tip

## Making Changes after Setting Up the Site

You can easily modify the information of a site you have defined previously.

❶ In the File panel, click on the drop-down site menu and select Manage Sites. This opens up the Manage Sites dialog box.

❷ Select your site and click [Edit]. This opens up the Site Definition dialog box. Make the changes and click [OK] to close the dialog box.

❸ Click [Done] to close the Manage Sites dialog box.

3. Click [Test]. A message box will pop up to tell you if you have succeeded in connecting to the remote server. Click [OK]. The remote site is now set up.

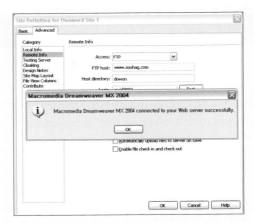

# Connecting to the Remote Site

1. After setting up the remote site, click the [Connects to Remote Host] icon () on the Files panel toolbar.

2. If you've set up the remote site correctly, you will see the contents of the remote site's host directory. Click the [Expand/Collapse] icon (▦) to expand the Files panel.

3. When expanded, the Files panel displays the contents of your site on the remote server on the left, and the contents of your site on your computer on the right. To return to the original view, click the [Expand/Collapse] icon (▦) to collapse the panel.

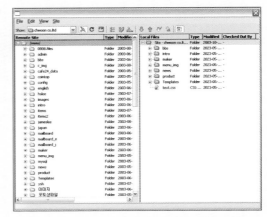

## Uploading a File to the Remote Site

After you have created a Web site, you need to make it available on the Web by uploading the files for the Web site onto the remote site. If you later make changes to some Web pages, you will need to update the Web site by uploading the amended files on the remote site.

1. Connect to the remote site.

2. Select a file from the local site list on the right window and click the [Put] icon (  ) on the Files panel toolbar. The Dependent Files dialog box appears. Dependent files are images and other files that are associated with the file you are uploading. If you are uploading a Web page to which you have added new images, for example, click [Yes]. Click [No] if you have only made modifications to the page's source code and not to the documents, images, or Flash files. This reduces the uploading time considerably.

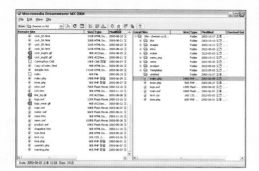

## Downloading a File from the Remote Site

If you need a copy of your Web site, you can download the files for your Web site from the remote site.

1. Connect to the remote site.

2. Select a file on the remote site list and click the [Get] icon ( ) on the Files panel toolbar. The Dependent Files dialog box appears. Click [Yes] to download all the files associated with the file you are downloading.

<< tip

### FTP Program

You need an FTP program for uploading and downloading files to and from the remote Web server. Although you can use an independent FTP program, the FTP program included in Dreamweaver MX 2004 is optimized for building Web sites and is a lot more convenient to use.

**Chapter** | 2

# Working with Text, Images, and Tables

The most common elements that can be found on Web pages are text, images, and tables. In this chapter, you will learn the basic techniques for working with these elements. You will also look at some real-life examples of how you can create simple Web pages using only these elements.

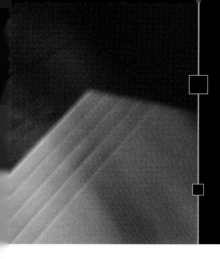

# Basic Techniques

Inserting and editing text, images, and tables are essential steps in the creation of almost any Web page, so becoming familiar with these basic techniques is vital. In this section, you will learn how to insert various elements into a Web page. You'll then learn how to edit them using the Properties Inspector.

## Selecting a View

Before you begin inserting elements into a Web page (or even start using Dreamweaver), you need to select a view to work in. Dreamweaver allows you to look at your work in both the Code View and Design View. The Code View shows the source code of a Web page while the Design View shows a Web page approximately as it would appear in a Web browser. The Split View shows both the Design View and the Code View at the same time. You can click on the [Design], [Split], or [Code] buttons in the Document window to select a view.

## Inserting Images

Inserting images in Dreamweaver is easy, but bear in mind that all images should be available on the local site. If the image you want to use is located elsewhere, copy it to the local site before inserting it into your Web page.

### Using the File Panel

If you have already defined a local site, using the File panel is probably the easiest way to insert images. Simply select the image you want from the File panel and drag it onto the workspace.

## Image File Formats Commonly Used in Web Pages

Small images with little color variation, such as buttons, menu bars, title images, and avatar icons, are usually stored in GIF format, while images with varying shades and tones, such as photographs, need to be in JPEG image format. The reason for this is that the GIF and JPEG formats are optimized according to color usage. The PNG format brings together the best of both worlds—the small size of GIF images and the abundant and rich color of JPEG images. But as PNG images do not show up properly in earlier versions of Web browsers, such as Netscape 3 and Internet Explorer 3, they are not as widely used as GIF and JPEG images. It will probably be several years before PNG becomes accepted as a widely used image format.

## Using the Insert Bar or Menu Bar

Select the [Common] tab on the Insert bar and click the [Image] button (🖾) or select [Insert] - [Image] from the menu bar at the top.  This opens the Select Image Source window. Select the image you want from the list. A preview of the image will be displayed. Click [OK] to insert the image.

## About the Image Properties Inspector

You can change the properties of an image using the Image Properties Inspector.

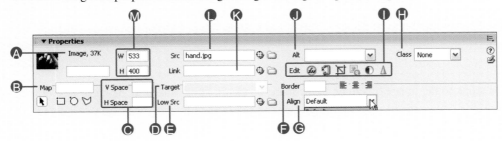

### Ⓐ Name

You should identify each image by giving it a name so that you can refer to it when applying behaviors or using a scripting language such as JavaScript (see Chapter 7).

### Ⓑ Map

This is used to divide an image into several sections, each with its own link.

### Ⓒ V Space and H Space

This adds space in pixels along the sides of an image. V Space adds space along the top and bottom while H Space adds space along the left and right sides of the image.

**Ⓓ Target**

After adding a link to an image, you can specify how you want the window for the linked page to appear. The options available are similar to those of the Target field for the Text Properties Inspector.

**Ⓔ Low Src**

For very large images, you should specify a low-resolution preview with a smaller file size that loads quickly and appears before the actual image finishes downloading. This is especially useful for users accessing your Web site using a slow connection.

**Ⓕ Border**

This sets the width of the image border in pixels.

**Ⓖ Align**

Click on the [Align Left], [Align Center], and [Align Right] buttons or choose an option from the Align pop-up menu to align an image with surrounding text. More information on this can be found in the note after this section.

**Ⓗ Class**

Select and apply style sheets from this menu. You will learn about style sheets in Chapter 3.

**Ⓘ Edit**

*Fireworks*: Click the [Edit] icon (⬤) to open the image in Fireworks, the default image editing program linked to Dreamweaver MX 2004.

*Optimize in Fireworks*: Click the [Optimize in Fireworks] icon (⬛) to optimize the image using Fireworks.

*Crop*: Click the [Crop] icon (⬛) to crop an image file. You can undo the crop command unless you quit Dreamweaver or edit the image using an external program. Before quitting Dreamweaver, it is a good idea to save a copy of the original image file in case you need to revert to the original size later on.

*Resample*: Click the [Resample] icon (⬛) to revert an image to its original size.

*Brightness/Contrast*: Click the [Brightness/Contrast] icon (⬛) to adjust the brightness and contrast of an image.

*Sharpen*: Click the [Sharpen] icon (⬛) to sharpen or blur an image.

**Ⓙ Alt**

You can type in a description for the image. This appears when you place your pointer over the image in the Web browser.

**Ⓚ Link**

You can add a link to the image by typing in the name of the file to be linked to. You can also drag the [Point to File] icon (⬛) to the file or click the [Browse for File] icon (⬛) to browse and select the file.

**Ⓛ Src**

This shows the current image path. You can change this by dragging the [Point to File] icon (⬛) to an image in the Files panel or by clicking the [Browse for File] icon (⬛) to browse and select the desired image.

**Ⓜ W and H (Width and Height)**

These set the width and height of the image in pixels.

## Aligning an Image with Surrounding Text

In order to align an image with its surrounding text, first select the image and then select an Align option from the Image Properties Inspector.

■ **Default/Baseline/Bottom**: Aligns the text to the bottom of the image. This is the default setting.

■ **Top**: Aligns the text to the top of the image.

■ **Middle**: Aligns the text to the center of the image.

■ **Text Top**: Aligns the top of the image with the tallest character in the text.

■ **Absolute Middle**: Aligns the center of the text to the center of the image.

■ **Absolute Bottom**: Aligns the base of the image with the lowest part of the text. For letters with descenders, such as q, g, and p, the bottom is at the lowest point of the 'tail.'

■ **Left**: Aligns the image to the left side of the text which is wrapped around it on the right.

■ **Right**: Aligns the image to the right side of the text which is wrapped around it on the left.

In the Design View, text can be entered directly into the Document window in a manner similar to many word processor programs. Dreamweaver allows you to look at your work in both Code View and Design View. The Code View shows the source code of a Web page while the Design View shows a Web page approximately as it would appear in a Web browser.

When text is entered in Design View, Dreamweaver automatically generates the code for that text on your Web page. To edit text after insertion, you can select the text you want to edit and make the changes in the Properties Inspector. If you are familiar with HTML coding, you can also modify the source code in the Code View.

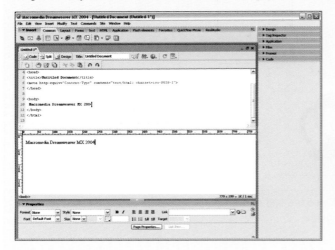

<< tip

**Adding Line Breaks and Paragraph Breaks**

To create a line break, press [Shift]-[Enter].
To create a paragraph break, press [Enter].

## About the Text Properties Inspector

The Text Properties Inspector enables you to easily format text on your Web pages.

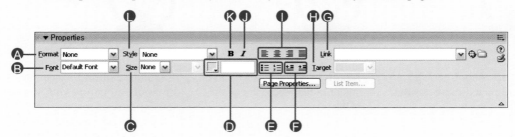

**Ⓐ Format**

You can apply or remove standard paragraph and heading formatting using this menu. To remove a paragraph format, select [None].

**Ⓑ Font**

By default, the Font pop-up menu includes only the more commonly used fonts so that your page will be accessible to a large audience. This list of fonts is editable and you may notice that the fonts are grouped in various combinations. More information on this can be found in the note at the end of this section.

**Ⓒ Size**

You can select an absolute font size from 9 to 36. You can also change a font size by selecting a description that ranges from xx-small to xx-large. These descriptions are applied in relation to the size of the selected text.

**Ⓓ Text Color**

Click the [Color] button (▣) to select a color from the palette. Alternatively, you can type in a color's hexadecimal code in the color text box (▭). This makes it easier for you to select a specific color.

**Ⓔ List**

Click the [Unordered List] icon (▤) to start a bulleted list, and the [Ordered List] icon (▤) if you want a numbered list. Hit [Enter] twice to end the list.

**Ⓕ Indent/Outdent**

Every click on these buttons will indent/outdent the line by one tab.

**Ⓖ Link**

You can add a link to selected text by typing in the name of the file to be linked to. You can also drag the [Point to File] icon (◉) to a file in the Site panel or click the [Browse for File] icon (▢) to browse and select the file.

**Ⓗ Target**

After inserting a link, you can specify how you want the window for the linked page to appear:

_blank: Opens the link in a new window.

_self: Opens the link in the current window.

_parent: Opens the link in the parent set of the current frame. (You will learn about frames in Chapter 4.)

_top: Opens the link in the current window.

**Ⓘ Alignment from Left to Right**

These buttons align the selected text to the left, center, or right–or justify the text on both sides.

**Ⓙ Italic**

Click this to italicize the selected text.

**Ⓚ Bold**

Click this to boldface the selected text.

**Ⓛ Style**

Dreamweaver automatically saves the formatting settings that you use on the different text elements on your Web page in the Style pop-up menu. These styles are generated each time you select a new set of formatting attributes for a text element.

## Font Combinations

The Font pop-up menu in the Text Properties Inspector contains a number of font combinations. The reason for selecting a combination of fonts instead of a single font is for accessibility. This enables the Web browser to use another font if one font is not available on the user's system.

Default Font
Arial, Helvetica, sans-serif
Times New Roman, Times, serif
Courier New, Courier, mono
Georgia, Times New Roman, Times, serif
Verdana, Arial, Helvetica, sans-serif
Geneva, Arial, Helvetica, sans-serif
serif, Arial, Courier
———————————
Edit Font List…

For example, if the first font in the combination, serif, is not available, the Web browser will display the Web page using the next font in the combination, Arial. If Arial is also not available, the page will be displayed in Courier.

## Adding a Font

1. To add a font, select [Edit Font List] from the Font pop-up menu in the Text Properties Inspector.

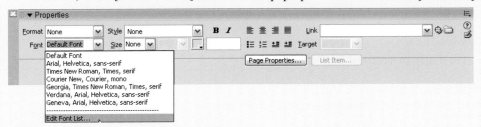

2. A dialog box appears, showing a list of available fonts. Select a font, click ⟨⟨, and then click [OK] to add the font. The font that you have just added will appear in the font list.

## Inserting Tables

Tables are an absolute necessity in modern Web page design, so you should practice using tables until you know them well. When working with tables, you can use either the Standard, Expanded Tables, or Layout modes. By default, Dreamweaver is set to display tables in the Standard mode. You can check or change the mode you are in by selecting the Layout menu in the Insert bar. You will see the [Standard], [Expanded Tables], and [Layout] mode buttons.

## Inserting Tables in Standard Mode

1. To insert a table in Standard mode, click the [Table] icon (▦) on the [Common] menu in the Insert bar.

2. The Table dialog box appears. Enter your settings and click [OK].

# About the Table Dialog Box

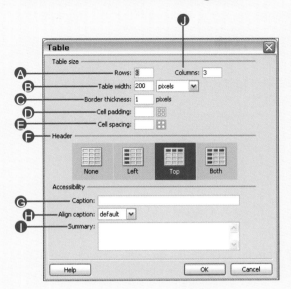

### A Rows

Type in the number of rows you want in the table.

### B Table width

You can specify how wide you want the table to be in pixels or percentage.

### C Border thickness

This sets the thickness of the cell's border. The default value is one pixel.

### D Cell padding

This is the space between the cell's content and its boundary in pixels. The default value is one pixel.

### E Cell spacing

This is the space between cells. The default value is one pixel.

### F Header

This bolds the text in the left column, the top row, or both. This option also aligns the content in the center of its cell. Select [None] if you don't want a header.

### G Caption

Enter the title for the table here.

### H Align caption

Aligns the caption in relation to the table.

### I Summary

Enter a description of the table here. This will be converted from text to speech if the user browses the Internet using screen readers. A screen reader is software for the visually impaired. The description will not appear in the Document window or the browser.

### J Columns

Type in the number of columns you want in the table

# About the Table Properties Inspector (Standard Mode)

To make modifications to a table using the Table Properties Inspector, make sure that the entire table is selected and not just a cell or a couple of cells.

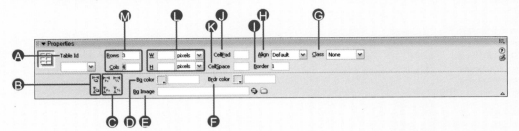

## A Table Id

Enter a name for the table here.

## B Clear Column Widths and Clear Row Heights

This removes unnecessary horizontal/vertical spacing from the cells so that the table contents will fit the border exactly.

## C Convert Table Widths/Heights to Pixels/Percent

Click one of these buttons to convert the width or height of the table into pixels, or a percentage of the browser window's width or height.

## D Bg color (Background Color)

Click the [Color] button (⬜) to select a background color for the table. You can also type in a color's hexadecimal code in the Color field (⬜). This makes it easier for you to select a specific color.

## E Bg Image (Background Image)

You can add a background image for the table by typing the name of the image file to be used. You can also drag the [Point to File] icon (⊕) to the file or click the [Browse for File] icon (▢) to browse and select the file.

## F Brdr color (Border Color)

For tables with borders, click the [Color Swatch] icon (⬜) to select a border color, or type in the hexadecimal color code in the Color Code field (⬜).

## G Class

You can select a style for the table.

## H Align

You can specify the alignment option for the table.

## I Border

This sets the width of the border for the table. The default value is one pixel.

## J CellPad

This sets the spacing between the cell contents and the cell border in pixels.

## K CellSpace

This sets the spacing between cells in pixels.

**Ⓛ W and H (Width and Height)**

This sets the width and height of the table, respectively.

**Ⓜ Rows and Cols**

This sets the number of rows and columns in the table, respectively.

## About the Cell Properties Inspector (Standard Mode)

When you select a cell, you can make more detailed modifications to the cell using the Cell Properties Inspector.

**Ⓐ Merge Cells**

Select two or more cells you want to merge. Then click the [Merge Cells] icon (▢) to merge the cells.

**Ⓑ Split Cell**

Select the cell you want to split and click the [Split Cell] icon (▤). The Split Cell dialog box appears. Specify the number of rows and/or columns you want to split the cells into and click [OK].

**Ⓒ Horz (Horizontal Alignment)**

This sets the horizontal alignment of images and text inside the cell.

**Ⓓ Vert (Vertical Alignment)**

This sets the vertical alignment of images and text inside the cell.

**Ⓔ W and H (Width and Height)**

You can adjust the width and height of the cell using these parameters.

**Ⓕ No wrap**

Select this option if you want the cell to adjust its width to accommodate text that is longer than the cell width. If this option is not selected, the cell will adjust vertically and wrap text.

**Ⓖ Header**

Select this option if you want to center and bold-face the text inside the cell to create a title.

**Ⓗ Bg (Background Image)**

You can add a background image for the cell by typing the name of the image file to be used. You can also drag the [Point to file] icon (⊕) to the file or click the [Browse for File] icon (▢) to browse and select the file.

**Ⓘ Bg (Background Color)**

Click the [Color Swatch] icon (▢) to select a background color for the cell. You can also type in the hexadecimal color code in the Color Code field (▭). This makes it easier for you to select a specific color.

**ⓙ Brdr (Border Color)**

For cells with borders, click the [Color Swatch] icon (▣) to select a border color, or type in the hexadecimal color code in the Color Code field (▭).

**ⓚ Page Properties**

Click here to set up page properties.

## Expanded Tables Mode

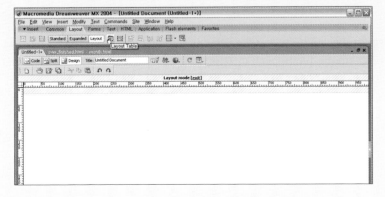

Standard Mode

Expanded Mode

The Expanded Tables mode is a new feature in Dreamweaver 2004 MX. In this mode, one pixel is added to the cell padding and spacing of all the cells to make editing easier. For example, you may want to switch to the Expanded mode if you want to place the insertion point next to an image inside a cell without accidentally selecting the image. The Expanded Tables mode does not reflect the actual visual appearance of the Web page. The extra space added to the cells only appears in the Design View; there is no real change to the cell or table size. As a rule, you should always revert to the Standard mode to edit and view the changes.

# Inserting Tables in Layout Mode

The Layout mode allows you to format your Web content very freely and easily, but it can result in very complicated tables. It is advisable to keep tables as simple and systematic as possible, or making changes can become very overwhelming. Before you can work on tables in Layout mode, you first need to switch to the Layout mode.

1. Click on the [Layout] tab of the Insert bar and click the [Layout] button (▣) to change to Layout View.

2. Click the [Layout Table] icon (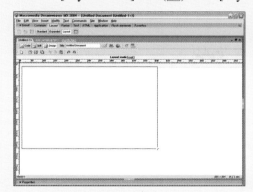) of the [Layout] menu. Click and drag in the work window to create a table.

3. Click the [Draw Layout Cell] icon () and drag the mouse inside the new table to create cells.  Repeat the step to add more cells.

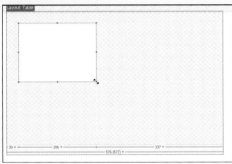

4. You can click on the border of these newly created cells to move the cells. You can also drag the border to change the size of the cells.

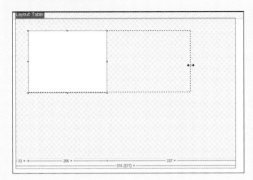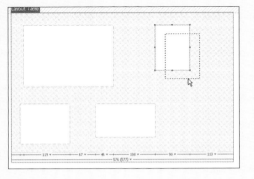

5. When you switch over to Standard mode, you will see that the table looks very complicated. It is nearly impossible to create such a complicated table in Standard mode. While the Layout mode gives you more flexibility, it may be better to simply create tables in Standard mode if they are fairly simple and regular.

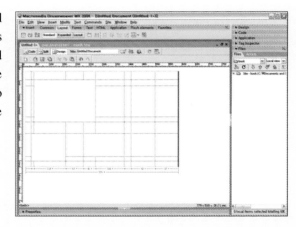

## About the Table Properties Inspector (Layout Mode)

You can easily modify the attributes of the table created in Layout mode using the Table Properties Inspector.

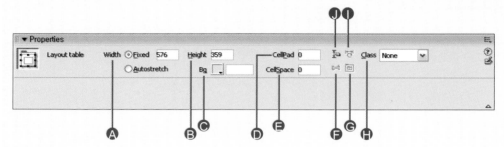

### Ⓐ Width

You can choose Fixed to set a fixed width and height, or Autostretch, which automatically stretches the window width to fit the size of the Web browser.

### Ⓑ Height

This sets the height of the table.

### Ⓒ Bg (Background Color)

Click the [Color Swatch] icon (⬚) to select a background color for the table. You can also type in the hexadecimal color code in the Color Code field (⬚). This makes it easier for you to select a specific color.

### Ⓓ CellPad

This sets the spacing between the cell contents and the cell border in pixels.

### Ⓔ CellSpace

This sets the spacing between cells in pixels.

### Ⓕ Remove All Spacers

Click this to remove all the transparent images that have been inserted to adjust spacing in the layout table.

### Ⓖ Remove Nesting

If you have created a table within a table and there is no data inside the inner table, click this option to remove the inner table.

**H Class**

You can select a style for the table.

**I Make Cell Widths Consistent**

If you have created a table within a table and the Autostretch option is activated for the outer table, this option allows the inner table to adjust to fit the size of the outer table.

**J Clear Row Heights**

Click this to remove excess spacing and adjust table heights.

## About the Cell Properties Inspector (Layout Mode)

When you select a cell in Layout mode, you can make more detailed modifications to the cell using the Cell Properties Inspector.

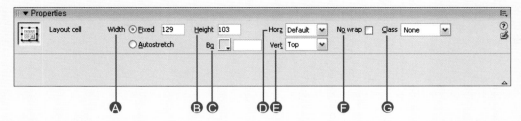

**A Width**

You can choose Fixed to set a fixed width for the cell or Autostretch, which automatically stretches the window width to fit the size of the Web browser.

**B Height**

This sets the height of the table.

**C Bg (Background Color)**

Click the [Color Swatch] icon (▦) to select a background color for the cell. You can also type in the hexadecimal color code in the Color Code field (▭). This makes it easier for you to select a specific color.

**D Horz (Horizontal Alignment)**

This sets the horizontal alignment of images and text inside the cell.

**E Vert (Vertical Alignment)**

This sets the vertical alignment of images and text inside the cell.

**F No wrap**

Select this option if you want the cell to adjust its width to accommodate text that is longer than the cell width. If this option is not selected, the cell will adjust vertically and wrap text.

**G Class**

You can select a style for the table.

# 1

# Making a Site Map

A site map provides visitors to a Web site with an overview of its structure, and is especially useful for larger Web sites. In this section, you will learn to create a site map using images to represent links to the various pages on the Web site, and tables to define the layout of the Web page.

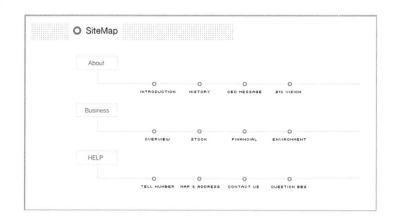

**Start File**
\Sample\Chapter02\Section01\sitemap.htm

**Final File**
\Sample\Chapter02\Section01\sitemap_finished.htm

**<< note**

**Resource Files**

Remember to copy the resource files on the CD-ROM to your local site before you start each exercise in this book.

Refer to Chapter 1 for more information on defining a local site and creating a new Web page.

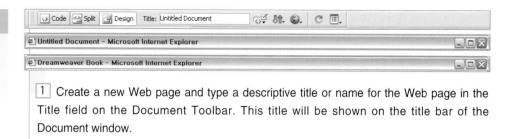

1 Create a new Web page and type a descriptive title or name for the Web page in the Title field on the Document Toolbar. This title will be shown on the title bar of the Document window.

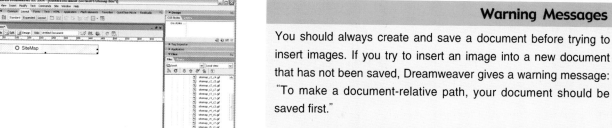

2 From the Files panel, drag the sitemap_ title.gif image from your local site onto the page. This image will serve as the title for the site map.

## Warning Messages

You should always create and save a document before trying to insert images. If you try to insert an image into a new document that has not been saved, Dreamweaver gives a warning message: "To make a document-relative path, your document should be saved first."

If you are inserting an image located outside the local site, a message will appear asking if you want to copy the file to the local site. Click [Yes]. When the Copy File As dialog box appears, create a new folder, name it **Images**, and save your image in it.

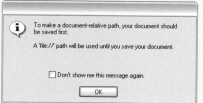

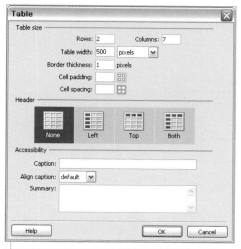

3 Place the insertion point below the image and click the [Table] (⊞) icon in the [Common] menu of the Insert bar to make a table with 2 rows and 7 columns. Set the width to 500 pixels and leave the border thickness at the default value of 1. Set Header to None.

## Planning Layouts Using Tables

The images used to form the About menu were created as a single image using image editing software, such as Fireworks or Photoshop. They were then cut into 8 portions to fit into a table with 2 rows and 7 columns. This method is commonly used in the creation of mastheads, navigation bars, and menus.

Before you start working on a Web page, you should decide how many tables you need and how many rows and columns these tables have. Using just one table for the entire Web page usually results in a very complex table that is difficult to edit and adjust. In the example for this section, 3 separate tables are created for the 3 menus so each can be edited independently.

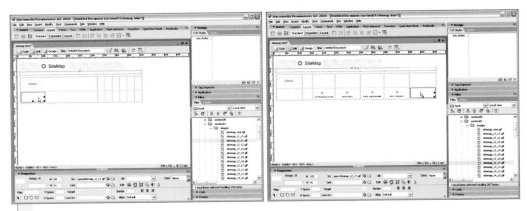

4 Click the top-left cell of the table. From the Files panel, drag sitemap_r1_c1.gif into the cell. Insert images into each of the remaining cells as shown below.

| sitemap_r 1_c1.gif | | | | | | |
|---|---|---|---|---|---|---|
| sitemap_r 2_c1.gif | sitemap_r 2_c2.gif | sitemap_r 2_c3.gif | sitemap_r 2_c4.gif | sitemap_r 2_c5.gif | sitemap_r 2_c6.gif | sitemap_r 2_c7.gif |

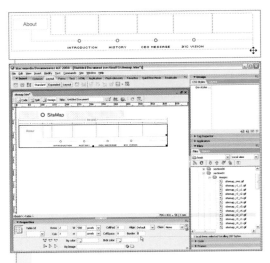

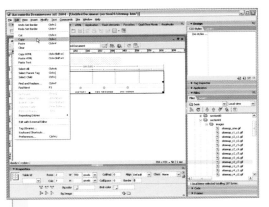

5 In this step, you will remove the space between the images so they look like a single unified image. To do so, you first have to select the table. Place the mouse over the table's border and click when the cursor changes to ( ⊕ ). After selecting the table, set CellPad, CellSpace, and Border to 0.

6 Now, you will make a copy of the first table for the Business menu. As the images for the About, Business, and Help menus are of the same dimensions, you can save quite a bit of time if you reuse the table. Select the table and click [Edit]-[Copy] from the menu bar at the top, or use the shortcut keys [Ctrl]-[C] to make a copy.

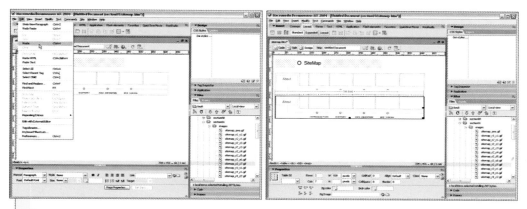

7   Click the area below the first table and select [Edit] - [Paste] from the pop-up menu to insert the copied table.

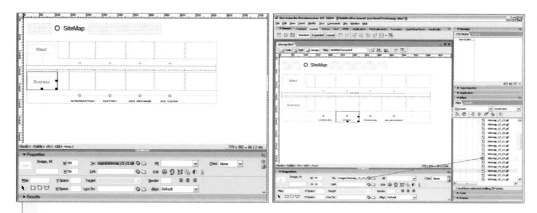

8   Now you just need to change the images in the second table to those created for the Business menu. You can do this by updating the images' source files in the Properties Inspector one by one. For example, you can select the top-left image, sitemap_r1_c1.gif, and change it to sitemap_r3_c1.gif. You can also change the source file using the [Point to File] icon (⊕) next to the Src field. First, select the sitemap_r2_c3.gif image. Then click on the [Point to File] icon (⊕) and drag it above the sitemap_r4_c3.gif image in the Files panel. This will change the image automatically. Using either method, change the remaining images accordingly.

| sitemap_r3_c1.gif | | | | | | |
|---|---|---|---|---|---|---|
| sitemap_r4_c1.gif | sitemap_r4_c2.gif | sitemap_r4_c3.gif | sitemap_r4_c4.gif | sitemap_r4_c5.gif | sitemap_r4_c6.gif | sitemap_r4_c7.gif |

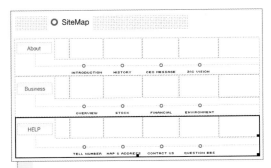

9 Repeat steps 6 to 8 to create the Help menu. Replace the images in the following order.

| sitemap_r 5_c1.gif | | | | | | |
|---|---|---|---|---|---|---|
| sitemap_r 6_c1.gif | sitemap_r 6_c2.gif | sitemap_r 6_c3.gif | sitemap_r 6_c4.gif | sitemap_r 6_c5.gif | sitemap_r 6_c6.gif | sitemap_r 6_c7.gif |

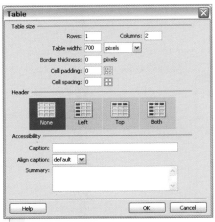

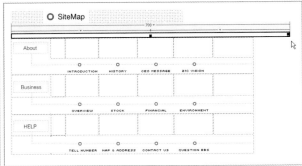

10 Note that the tables are too close to the left border. You can adjust the layout by creating a new table and embedding the menu tables in the second column, leaving the first column empty. This empty column will shift the menu tables to the right. First of all, select all 3 tables and press [Ctrl]-[C] to copy them. Click the bottom of the Site Map image and click the Table icon (⊞) on the Insert bar. The Table dialog box appears. Set Rows to 1 and Columns to 2.

<< note

## Copy-and-Paste vs Cut-and-Paste

Although you could cut and paste the three tables, it is always safer to copy and paste the tables so you will have a backup copy in case anything goes wrong along the way.

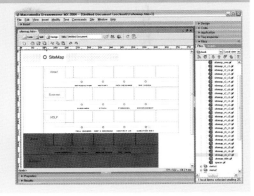

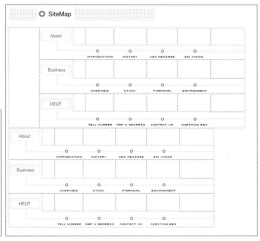

11  For the new table, select the left cell and set its width to 100 pixels in the Cell Properties Inspector. Select the right cell and set its width to 600 pixels. Left-click the mouse on the right cell and press [Ctrl]-[V] to paste the 3 menu tables.

12  If you are satisfied with the three cells you have inserted, select the tables at the bottom and select [Edit] - [Clear] from the menu bar at the top. In this exercise, you have moved three tables to the right by 100 pixels while keeping them aligned using embedded tables. This technique is extremely useful in positioning and aligning tables on Web pages.

<< note

## Adjusting Blank Spaces

To change the dimensions of a cell in an embedded table, you need to change the dimensions of both the cell and the outer table. For example, if you wish to widen the left column of the Site Map example by another 100 pixels, you need to increase both the left cell width and the outer table width by 100.

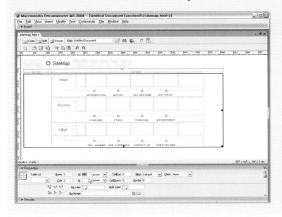

# Exercise 2

# Creating a Favorites List

Using lists to present information is a great way of breaking the monotony of lengthy paragraphs. It highlights the important points and makes a Web page more readable. A list that arranges items by number is called an ordered list. You can also create lists where the items are bulleted but not numbered. These are called unordered lists. In this section, you will learn how to create an ordered list of favorite albums.

**Start File**

\Sample\Chapter02\Section02\mp3.htm

**Final File**

\Sample\Chapter02\Section02\mp3_finished.htm

<< note

## Resource Files

Remember to copy the resource files on the CD-ROM to your local site before you start each exercise in this book.

1 First, select [Modify] - [Page Properties]. Specify the title for the Web page by typing **mp3** in the Title field. Then click the [Browse] button next to the Background Image field. The Select Image Source dialog box appears. Select the doc_bg.gif file from the appropriate folder on your local site. In the Image Preview window, you will see that doc_bg.gif is a long thin strip of 1200 pixels by 10 pixels. The height only needs be 10 pixels because background images are tiled repeatedly so they cover the entire page. Click [OK].

2 At the Page Properties dialog box, set both the left and top margins to 0 to remove all spacing. Click [OK]. Note that the cursor is now at the top-left corner of the Design View window. Select [File] - [Save As] and save the file as **music.htm**.

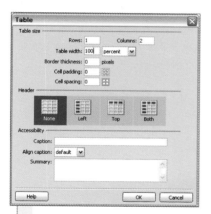

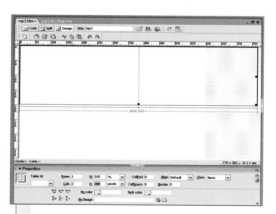

3 Click the [Table] icon (▦) of the [Common] menu in the Insert bar and create a table with 1 row and 2 columns. In the Table dialog box, set Table Width to 100% so that the table will expand to fit the Web browser's window. Set the values for Cell padding, Cell spacing, and Border thickness to 0. Click [OK].

4 As the background image you will be inserting in the next step is 200 pixels in height, you need to adjust the table to fit the image. To do this, select the table and—in the Properties Inspector—set H to 200 pixels. Note that you can also adjust the height of the table after inserting the image.

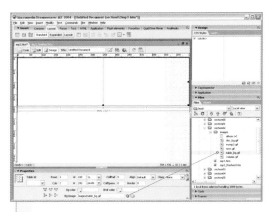

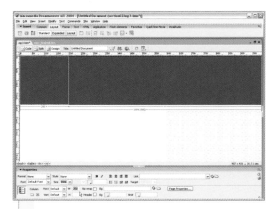

**5** Select the table and—in the Properties Inspector—click and drag the [Point to File] icon (⊕) next to [Bg Image] over the Table_bg.gif image in the Files panel to insert the image.

**6** Select the left cell by holding down the [Ctrl] key and clicking the cell. In the Properties Inspector, set W to 200. This will automatically be recognized as 200 pixels.

<< note

## Making a Variable Table

A variable table is one in which the size is set to 100% so that the width of the table always stretches to fit any and all browser environments. In this exercise, the left cell is fixed at 200 pixels while the right cell is variable so it can adjust according to the browser window size. This technique is commonly used in creating mastheads.

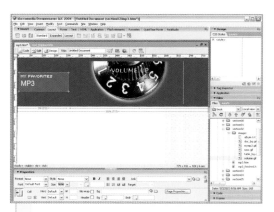

**7** Click and drag the mymp3.gif image from the Files panel into the left cell. Then click and drag the volume.gif image from the Files panel into the right cell.

**8** Select the right cell by holding down the [Ctrl] key and clicking the cell. In the Properties Inspector, set Vert to top. This aligns the image to the top of the cell.

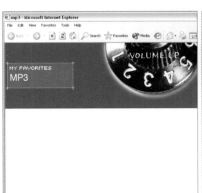

9 | Press [F12] to preview your work in the Web browser. Change the size of the browser window and observe how the left cell remains unchanged while the right cell changes in size to fit the changing browser.

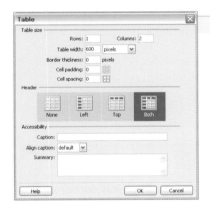

10 | Now it's time to insert the album title image. Place the insertion point at the bottom of the masthead. Click the [Table] icon (⊞) of the [Command] menu in the Insert bar and create a 600-pixel table with 1 row and 2 columns. In the Table dialog box, set the values for the Cell padding, Cell spacing, and Border thickness to 0. Click [OK].

11 | Select the left cell by holding down the [Ctrl] key and clicking the cell. In the Properties Inspector, set W to 100.

12 | Click the right cell and drag the new.gif image from the Files panel into the cell. Note that a 100-pixel margin is created on the left-hand side of the image.

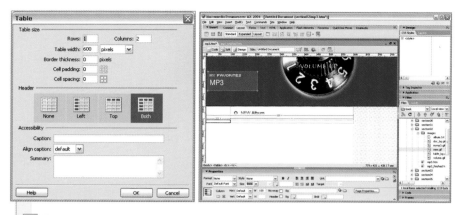

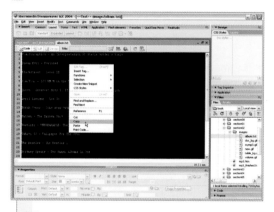

13 Repeat step 12 to create another table of the same dimensions. You will use this new table for inserting the actual music list.

14 In the Files panel, double-click on the album.txt file on your local site to open it in a new document window. Press [Ctrl]-[A] to select the entire text and right-click the mouse and select [Copy] from the short-cut menu that appears.

15 Click the mp3.htm tab at the upper-left corner of the Document window to switch to the Web page.

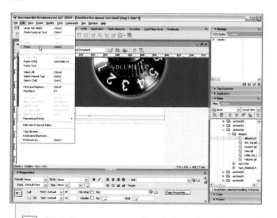

<< note

### Selecting an Active File

If you have several files open on the desktop at the same time, you can see which files are open by looking at the tabs in the upper left-hand corner. Click on the tab of the file you need to access the file quickly.

16 Click the mouse on the right cell and select [Edit] - [Paste] from the pop-up menu to paste the copied text. This inserts the copied text into the cell.

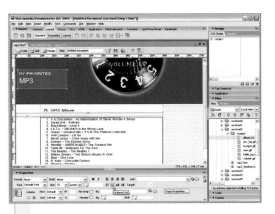

17 Select the right cell by holding down the [Ctrl] key and clicking the cell. Click the [Ordered List] icon (📋) in the Properties Inspector. As the text appears a little too big, you should set the text size to 10 points.

<< note

## Common Font Size on the Web

The body texts of most Web pages are set to size 10, the standard font size for the Windows OS (98, 2000, XP) environment.

18 Press [F12] to preview your work in the Web browser.

<< note

## Changing Between Ordered and Unordered Lists

To convert an ordered list to an unordered one, select the desired list and click on the [Unordered List] icon (📋) in the Properties Inspector. Likewise, you can change an unordered list into an ordered one by selecting the list and then clicking on the [Ordered List] icon (📋) in the Properties Inspector.

# Producing Different Layouts with Tables

Tables are extremely flexible and can be used to produce all kinds of layouts by nesting tables within tables and by adjusting parameters such as cell padding, cell spacing, and border thickness. In this section, you will learn how to produce different layout designs by manipulating table parameters.

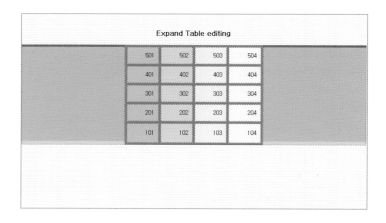

**Start File**
\Sample\Chapter02\Section03\apt.htm

**Final File**
\Sample\Chapter02\Section03\apt_finished.htm

<< note

### Resource Files

Remember to copy the resource files on the CD-ROM to your local site before you start each exercise in this book.

1 Open the apt.htm file. Click the [Page Properties] button in the Properties Inspector to open the Page Properties dialog box.

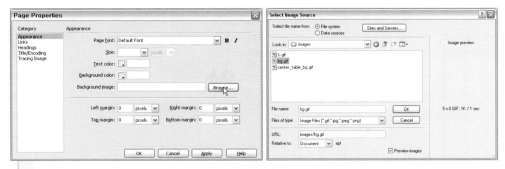

2 Click [Browse] in the Page Properties dialog box. The Select Image Source dialog box appears. Select the bg.gif file from your local site. Click [OK]. This inserts the file as a background image. When you return to the Page Properties dialog box, click [OK].

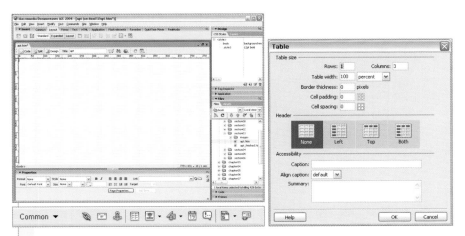

3 Click the [Table] icon (⊞) of the [Common] menu in the Insert bar to create a table. In the Table dialog box, set Rows to 1 and Columns to 3. Click [OK].

4 Select the table and—in the Properties Inspector—set W to 100% and H to 230 pixels.

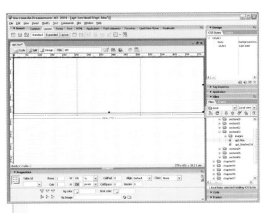

5 Select the leftmost cell by holding down the [Ctrl] key and clicking the cell. In the Properties Inspector, set W to 30%. Repeat with the middle and rightmost cells, setting their widths to 40% and 30%, respectively.

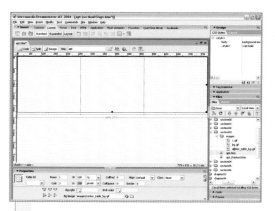

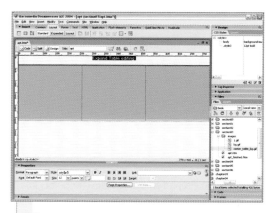

6  Next, select the entire table. Then click and drag the [Point to File] icon (⊕) to the center_table_bg.gif file to select it as the background image.

7  Place the insertion point at the top of the Document window and add a few lines of text. Select the entire text. In the Properties Inspector, set Style to Style3 and click the [Bold] button to boldface the text.

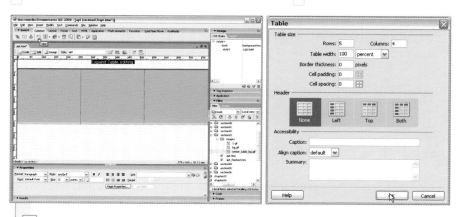

8  Click inside the middle cell and click the [Table] icon (▦) to insert a table. When the Table dialog box appears, set the number of rows and columns to 5 and 4, respectively. Set Table Width to 100%.

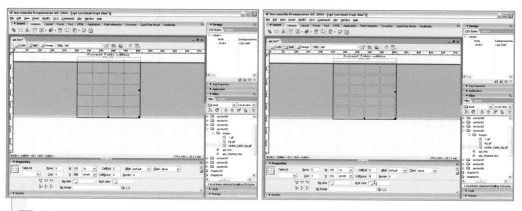

9  Select the table inside the middle cell. In the Properties Inspector, set Cell spacing to 5. Keep the height of the table at 230 pixels. You should be able to see that the spacing inside the cells has increased somewhat.

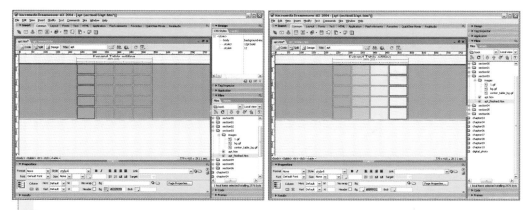

**10** Select one column of cells at a time and make each column a different color. Try to use only light colors.

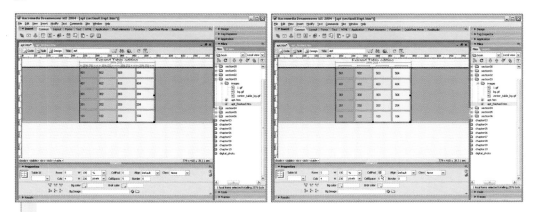

**11** Type a different apartment number for each of the table compartments. Select the <table> tag at the bottom of the Document window to select the embedded table. In the Properties Inspector, set Cell padding to 10. This makes the numbers appear farther apart from each other.

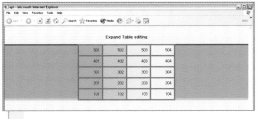

**12** Select the <td> tag at the bottom of the Document window. This selects both the inner and outer tables. In the Properties Inspector, type #339999 in the background color field. This changes the cell spacing to a bright cyan color.

**13** Press [F12] to preview your work in the Web browser.

<< tip

## Nested Table Technique

The nested table technique is frequently used to lay out web pages. By using different levels of nesting and adjusting parameters such as cell spacing, cell padding, and border thickness, different visual effects can be achieved easily.

# Creating Rollover Effects

One of the most effective ways of indicating active elements on Web pages is to introduce rollover effects. When the cursor moves over an active image, it changes to another image, giving an instant visual cue to the user. Rollover effects are also great for jazzing up Web pages. In this section, you will learn how to create simple rollover effects using Dreamweaver.

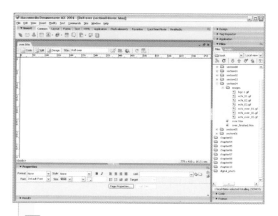

**Start File**

\Sample\Chapter02\Section04\over.htm

**Final File**

\Sample\Chapter02\Section04\over_finished.htm

<< note

## Resource Files

Remember to copy the resource files on the CD-ROM to your local site before you start each exercise in this book.

1 Open the over.htm file. Click the [Page Properties] button in the Properties Inspector to open the Page Properties dialog box.

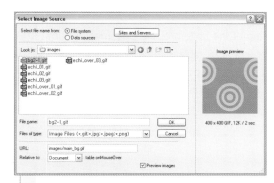

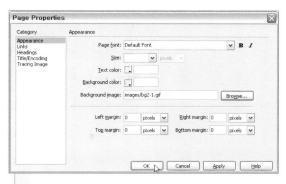

2 Click the [Browse in the Page Properties] button. The Select Image Source dialog box appears. Select the bg2-1.gif file from your local site. Click [OK]. This inserts the file as a background image and returns to the Page Properties dialog box.

3 In the Page Properties dialog box, set Left, Right, Top, and Bottom margins to 0. Click [OK].

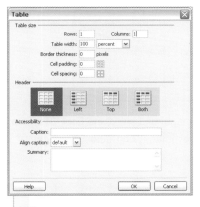

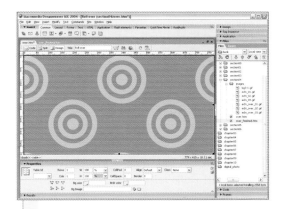

4 Click the [Table] icon (⊞) of the [Common] menu in the Insert bar to create a table. In the Table dialog box, set both Rows and Columns to 1. Set Table Width to 100% and click [OK].

5 Select the entire table and set H in the Properties window to 100%. This creates a table that fills up the entire page, as shown here.

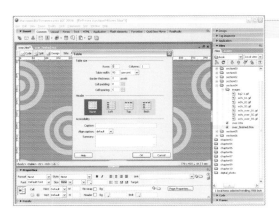

6 Click inside the table and then click the [Table] icon (⊞) to insert a table within. When the Table dialog box appears, set both Rows and Columns to 1. Set Table Width to 80%.

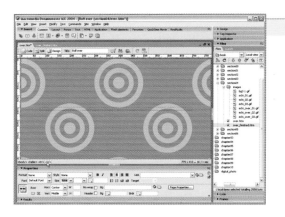

7 Select the <td> tag at the bottom of the Document window. This selects both the inner and outer tables. In the Properties Inspector, set both Horz and Vert to center. This positions the nested table at the center of the outer table, no matter what the size of the browser window is.

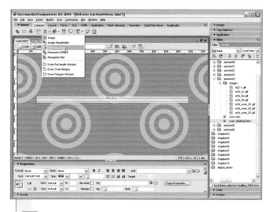

8 Click inside the second table. Then click the [Image] icon ( ) of the [Common] menu in the Insert bar. In the pull-down menu, select Rollover Image. The Insert Rollover Image dialog box appears.

9 Click [Browse for Original Image] and select the Echi_01.gif file. Next, click [Browse for Rollover Image] and select the Echi_01_over.gif file. Click [OK].

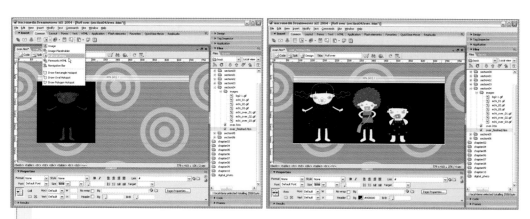

10 Repeat steps 8 and 9 for 2 more original images, Echi_02.gif and Echi_03.gif. Their rollover images are Echi_02_over.gif and Echi_03_over.gif, respectively.

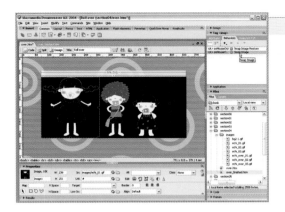

11 Select the first image and click the Behavior panel under the Tag Inspector panel group. This Behavior panel contains events such as onMouseOver and onMouseOut that you can assign to rollover images. Select onMouseOver. Repeat for the other 2 images.

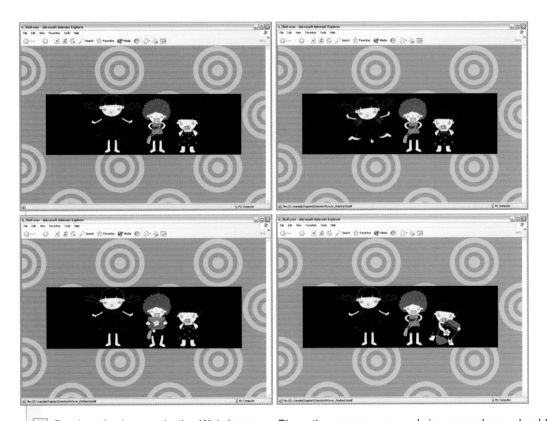

12 Preview the images in the Web browser. Place the cursor over each image and you should be able to see the rollover effect.

# 5

# Making a Calendar

Besides organizing lists and images, tables are also great for creating tabulated items such as calendars and schedules. In this section, you will learn how to use embedded tables to make a customized calendar for the month of December, 2004.

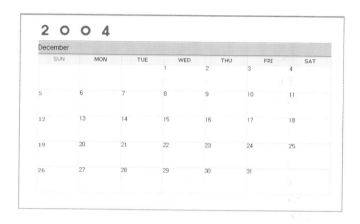

## Start File
\Sample\Chapter02\Section05\month.htm

## Final File
\Sample\Chapter02\Section05\month_finished.htm

<< note

## Resource Files

Remember to copy the resource files on the CD-ROM to your local site before you start each exercise in this book.

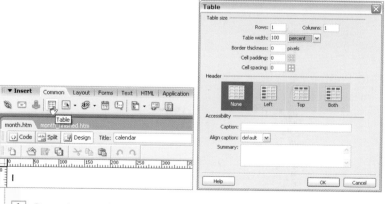

1 Open the month.htm file. Click the [Table] icon (▦) of the [Common] menu in the Insert bar to create a table. In the Table dialog box, set both Rows and Columns to 1. Set Table Width to 100%. Click [OK].

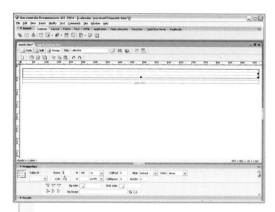

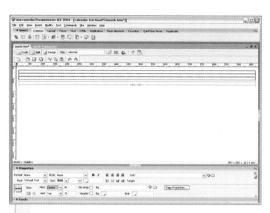

2  Select the entire table. In the Properties Inspector, set Rows to 3. This increases the number of rows in the table to 3. Note that this step is intended only to illustrate the technique of changing the number of rows in a table after it has been created. Under normal circumstances, you should specify the desired number of rows when you create the table.

3  Select all the cells of the table. In the Properties Inspector, set Horz to Center and Vert to Top. This positions the nested table at the center of the outer table, no matter what the size of the browser window. All data entered will start from the top down.

4  Select the entire table. In the Properties Inspector, set W to 700 pixels.

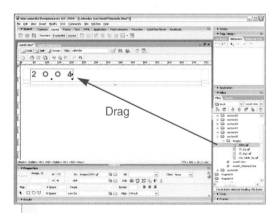

5  Drag the 2004.gif file from your local folder into the table.

6  Click inside the second cell and click the [Table] icon (▦) to insert a table. When the Table dialog box appears, set Table Width to 700 pixels. Click [OK].

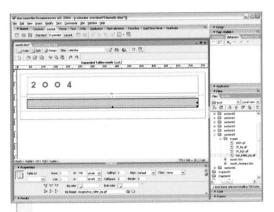

7 Select the table inside the second cell. In the Properties Inspector, set Bg Image to the top_table_bg.gif file.

8 Repeat step 6 with the third cell. Select the table inside the third cell. In the Properties Inspector, set Bg color to #C6D7D7.

9 Click the [Layout] tab of the Insert bar and click the [Expanded] button ( Expanded ) to change to the Expanded Tables mode. In this mode, cell paddings and spacings of 1 pixel are added to all cells so the table's borders are increased, making editing easier. It is also easier to see the structure of the table in the Expanded Tables mode. As the Expanded Tables mode does not reflect the actual visual appearance of the Web page, remember to revert to the Standard mode by clicking the [Standard] button ( Standard ) before proceeding.

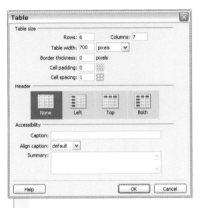

10 Click inside the third cell and click the [Table] icon ( ▦ ) to insert a table. When the Table dialog box appears, set Rows and Columns to 6 and 7. Set the Table Width to 700 pixels and Cell Spacing to 1. The increased cell spacing allows the background color applied in step 8 to show through.

11 Select all the cells of the inserted table. In the Properties Inspector, set Bg to white.

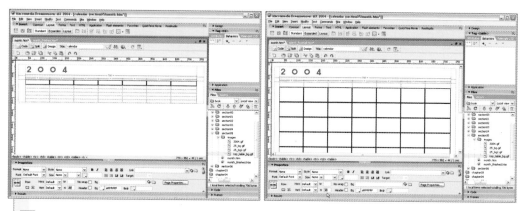

**12** Select the first row of cells in the table. In the Properties Inspector, set H to 20. Select the remaining rows of cells and set H to 60.

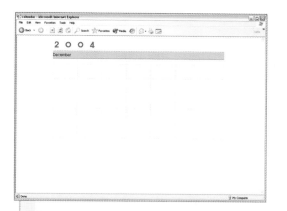

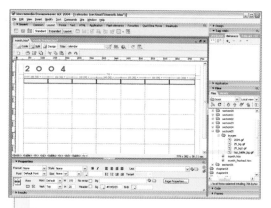

**13** Press [F12] to preview your work in the Web browser. Note how the cell spacing creates the effect of a table with white cells and a thin cyan border.

**14** Select the first row of cells for the embedded table inside the third cell. In the Properties Inspector, set Bg color to #D9EDED.

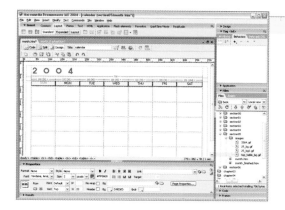

**15** Place the insertion point in the first cell of the embedded table inside the third cell. Type **SUN** (for Sunday). Repeat for the remaining cells in the same row, typing in the names of the days of the week.

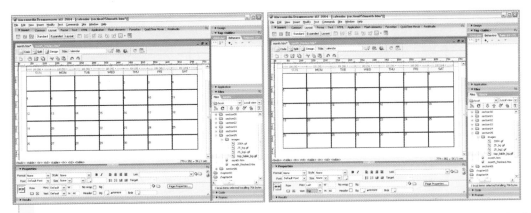

16 Place the insertion point in the appropriate cells and type in the dates pertaining to the month of December, 2004. Then select all the white cells and, in the Properties Inspector, set Horz to Left and Vert to Top.

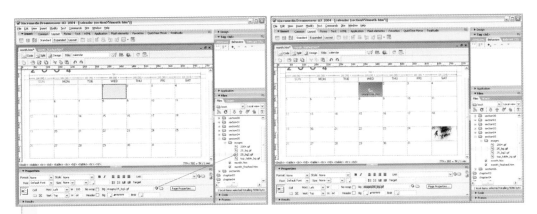

17 You can apply different background images to specific cells to highlight special days. Select the cell for December 1st and drag the [Bg Point to File] icon to the 25_bg2.gif file on the local site. Next, select the cell for December 25th and drag the [Bg Point to File] icon to the 25_bg.gif file.

<< note

## Image Name

Always label your images with meaningful names so you can identify and retrieve them easily. Otherwise, you will need to open up each one to find out what it is.

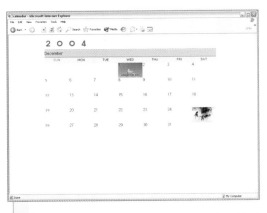

18 Press [F12] to preview your December 2004 calendar in the Web browser.

# 6 Producing an Office Arrangement in Layout Mode

Regular tables can easily be done in Standard mode, but if the positions of the tables are irregular, or even haphazard, Layout mode will certainly make life much easier. It is thus important that you know how to choose the most appropriate mode in which to work. In this section, you will explore the Layout mode further by creating the layout of an office.

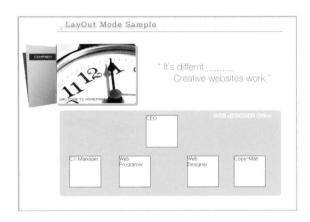

**Start File**
\Sample\Chapter02\Section06\office.htm

**Final File**
\Sample\Chapter02\Section06\office_finished.htm

<< note
## Resource Files

Remember to copy the resource files on the CD-ROM to your local site before you start each exercise in this book.

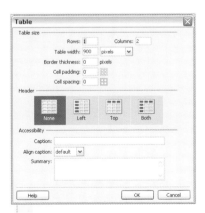

1 Open the office.htm file. Click the [Table] icon (⊞) of the [Common] menu in the Insert bar to create a table. In the Table dialog box, set Rows to 1 and Columns to 2. Set Table Width to 900 pixels and click [OK].

2 Select the left cell. In the Properties Inspector, set W to 120 pixels. Then select the right cell. In the Properties Inspector, set W to 780 pixels.

3 Select the entire table and select [Edit] - [Copy] from the menu to copy. Then select [Edit] - [Paste] to paste the table. Repeat so you end up with a total of 3 tables.

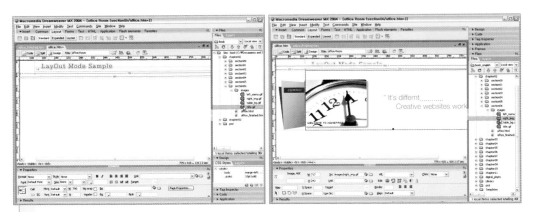

4 Drag the title.gif file from your local folder into the right cell of the topmost table. Then drag the left_menu.gif and right_img.gif from your local folder into the left and right cells of the second table.

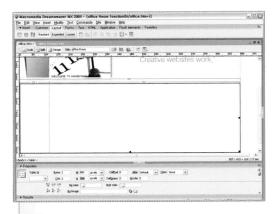

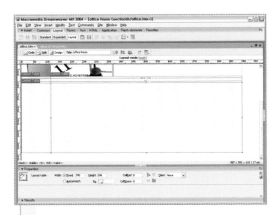

5 Select the bottommost table and—in the Properties Inspector—set H to 286 pixels, which is the size of the background image to be inserted there.

6 Click the [Layout] tab of the Insert bar and click the [Layout] button ( Layout ) to change to Layout mode. Click on the [Layout Table] icon (  ) and then drag the mouse across the window to create a table that is the same size as the cell on the right.

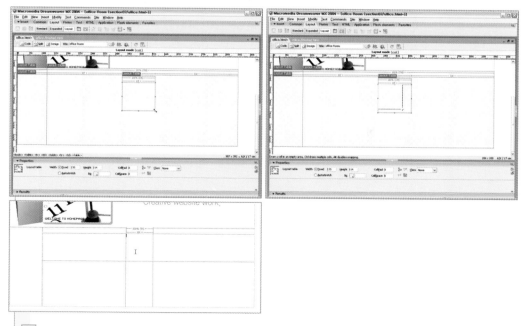

7 Click on the [Layout Table] icon ( ) and drag the mouse to create a smaller table inside the one created in the previous step. Now, click on the [Draw Layout Cell] icon ( ) and drag the mouse over the new table to draw a cell of the same size. If you go to the Standard mode, you will see that Dreamweaver has generated a table to accommodate the new tables you specified.

<< tip

## Moving Tables

It is easier to move tables in Layout mode than in Standard mode. It is also easier to adjust the size of tables in Layout mode using the markers.

8 In the Layout mode, create a few more tables with cells of the same size. You can move a table to another location by clicking the title of the table and dragging it to the new position.

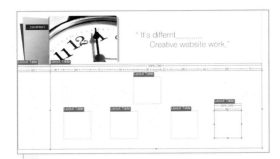

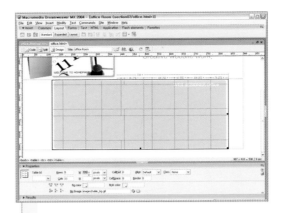

9 Select one of the newly created tables. In the Properties Inspector, select Fixed for the width value and set it to 100 pixels. Repeat for the other embedded tables.

10 Click the [Layout] tab of the Insert bar and click the [Standard] button ( Standard ) to change to Standard mode. Select the <table> tag at the bottom of the Document window. This selects the table containing the smaller tables. In the Properties Inspector, set Bg Image to the tagle_bg.gif file.

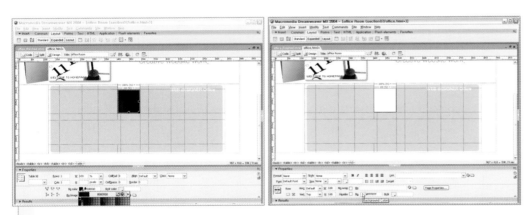

11 Select one of the newly created tables. In the Properties Inspector, change Bg to black. Next, select the cell of that table by clicking the inner <td> tag at the bottom of the Document window. In the Properties Inspector, set Bg to white. Set Cell spacing to 1 and make sure W is set to 100 pixels, not 100%. Note that switching between Standard and Layout modes can cause the initially set value of 100 pixels to be changed to 100%. To rectify this, simply change the unit of measurement back to percent.

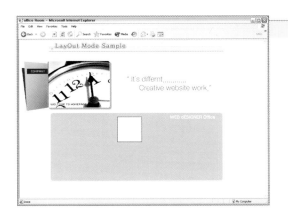

12 Press [F12] to preview your work in the Web browser. Note that the table now has a border. This is because the background colors for the table and the cell are different. Adding a cell spacing of 1 allows a line to show up—which looks like a border.

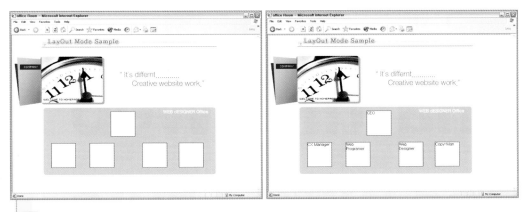

13 Repeat step 11 for all the 5 tables created in the Layout mode. Type in the relevant texts and preview your work in the Web browser.

Chapter | 3

# Formatting Web Pages with Style Sheets

Styles sheets are formatting definitions that can quickly and effortlessly modify the appearance of Web pages. Although the basic theory behind style sheets has not changed much from its simple beginning, the functionalities and capabilities of style sheets have grown significantly. In this chapter, you will learn how to create different types of style sheets and use them in Web pages.

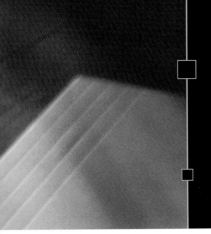

# Introduction to Style Sheets

Style sheets are like templates that you can use to format various Web elements such as text, tables, and layers. They are thus especially popular for formatting large Web sites, defining styles for almost any Web page element. With Web sites becoming larger and more complex, it is almost unthinkable to work without style sheets.

## About Style Sheets

Style sheets are also known as Cascading Style Sheets, or CSS. If you have a huge Web site with several hundred pages, you can easily use style sheets to set the font, font size, and text color on all the pages at one go instead of manually formatting each page.

If you decide to make any changes to the formatting, such as the font size, you will only need to modify the appropriate style sheet and the changes will be reflected in all the Web elements to which the style has been applied. This enables you to make site-wide changes quickly. The larger the Web site, the more you will be able to appreciate what style sheets can do.

## Creating a Style Sheet

You can create two types of style sheets: internal and external. Internal style sheets are saved on a Web page while external style sheets are saved as separate files.

### Internal Style Sheet

Internal style sheets can only be applied to the page in which they are embedded. The code for an internal style can be seen in Code View where you can directly edit the tags.

1. Click on the [New CSS Style] icon (⊞) in the CSS Styles panel. The New CSS Style dialog box appears.

2. Name the style sheet **.rexText**. Select [This Document Only] under Define In and then click [OK]. The CSS Style Definition dialog box will appear.

<< **tip**

## Naming Style Sheets

When naming a style sheet, you are only allowed to use Roman letters and no special symbols or signs. If you try to give a style sheet a name that has a space, symbol, or sign, a dialog box will appear asking you to remove the unacceptable characters. All style sheet names are preceded by a period. You can enter the period yourself or leave it to Dreamweaver to add it in.

3. Under Category, select Type and set the color to red. Click [OK].

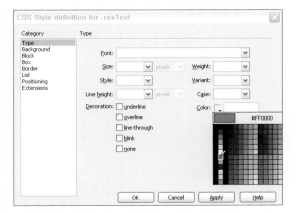

4. In the CSS Styles panel, you can see that the .rexText style has been added. If you double-click on the style, the Tag Inspector will turn into the Rule ".rexText" panel and you will see the style settings in the CSS Properties tab.

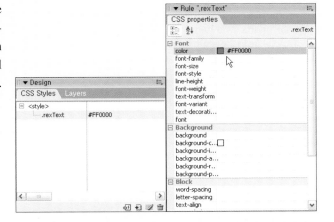

5. Type in a word on the page. In the Properties Inspector, click on the Style pop-up menu and select the .rexText style to apply it. Styles are applied to text one paragraph at a time and, in the case of tables, one cell at a time.

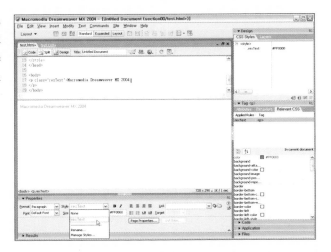

6. Switch to Code View or double-click on the style in the CSS Styles panel to view the code for the style which has been embedded with the page. You can also double-click on the style in the Tag Inspector or the Rule ".rexText" panel to view the code.

```
1  <!DOCTYPE HTML PUBLIC "-//W3C//DTD HTML 4.01 Transitional//EN"
2  "http://www.w3.org/TR/html4/loose.dtd">
3  <html>
4  <head>
5  <title>Untitled Document</title>
6  <meta http-equiv="Content-Type" content="text/html; charset=euc-kr">
7  <style type="text/css">
8  <!--
9  .rexText {
10     color: #FF0000;
11 }
12 -->
13 </style>
14 </head>
15
16 <body>
17 <p class="rexText">Macromedia Dreamweaver MX 2004
18 </p>
19 </body>
20 </html>
21
```

## Applying a Style Sheet

You can also apply a style by using the CSS Styles panel or the Tag Selector. Before you try out the steps below, you should first select the element you want to change in the Design View.

■ Using the CSS Styles Panel
In the CSS Styles panel, right-click on the style name and select [Apply] from the shortcut menu.

■ Using the Tag Selector
Right-click on the tag for the element you want to modify in the Tag Selector. Select the [Set Class] command from the shortcut menu and choose a style.

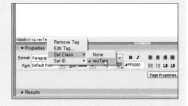

# About the CSS Styles Panel

The CSS Styles panel lets you create, edit, and manage style sheets.

When you have style sheets on your Web page, you will see the CSS style properties on the right side of the panel.

78

**Ⓐ Attach Style Sheet (⊞):** Imports or links to an external style sheet.

**Ⓑ New CSS Style (⊞):** Creates a new internal or external style sheet.

**Ⓒ Edit Style Sheet (✎):** Provides several options for editing the selected style sheet.

**Ⓓ Delete CSS Style (🗑):** Deletes the style sheet.

## External Style Sheet

If your Web site has many pages that use a similar layout, it will be very tedious to apply the same style to each page one by one. To overcome this, Dreamweaver allows you to define an external style in a separate file and then apply it to different pages. When you modify an external style, the changes will automatically be reflected on all the pages to which the style has been applied.

1. In the CSS Styles panel, click the [New CSS Style] icon (⊞). When the New CSS Style dialog box appears, name the style **.text**. Under the Define In options, select [New Style Sheet File] and click [OK].

2. The Save Style Sheet File As dialog box appears. Select the local folder into which you wish to save the style. Type a name for your new style file and click [OK]. It is important to have your local site defined first before trying to saving a style file. Otherwise, the style may not work properly.

3. The CSS Style Definition dialog box appears. Change Font to [Arial, Helvetica, Sans-Serif], Size to 9 points, and type **#666666** in the Color field. Click [OK].

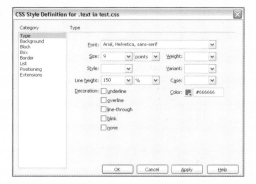

4. You can see that the text.css file has been created in the Design, Rule, and Files panels.

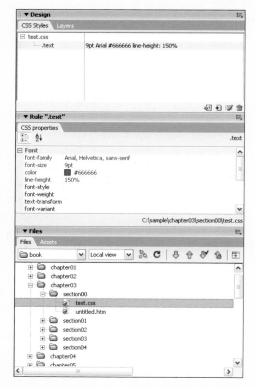

## Linking to an External Style Sheet

You can add an external style sheet to a Web site by either linking or importing the style sheet file. Because the difference between the steps for linking and importing an external style sheet is only in selecting the Link or Import option from a dialog box, this exercise covers only the exact steps for linking to an external style sheet. In the steps that follow, you will also learn about the difference between linking and importing an external style sheet.

1. In the Files panel, select the section00 folder and right-click to open the shortcut menu. Select [New File] to create a new file. Name it **abc.htm**.

2. In the CSS Styles panel, click the [Attach Style Sheet] icon (). The Attach External Style Sheet dialog box appears. Under the Add as options, select Link. Click [Browse] to look for the style sheet you wish to link. Select text.css from the section00 folder and click [OK]. This links the text.css style sheet to abc.htm.

<< tip

## Import vs Link

When you import an external style sheet, Dreamweaver duplicates the tags as an internal style, but if you link to a style sheet, the tags are not copied in. The Web page simply refers to the external style files for style information.

3. Click the [Code View] button () and examine the source code. Note the line that reads <link href="text.css" rel="stylesheet" type="text/css"> in the tag. You should see the style in the CSS Styles and Rule panels.

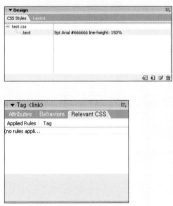

# Designing an Investor Relations Page

It can be quite overwhelming to browse through a vast amount of numerical data on a Web page, so proper organization and presentation is extremely important. Aligning and formatting such data manually can be very tiresome, but with the help of tables and style sheets, the task is considerably easier. In this section, you will learn to align and format data on a Web page.

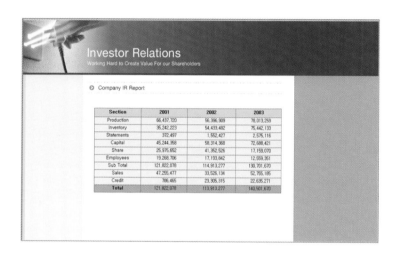

**Start File**

\Sample\Chapter03\Section01\ir.htm

**Final File**

\Sample\Chapter03\Section01\ir_finished.htm

1 Open the ir.htm file. It contains a table of numbers.

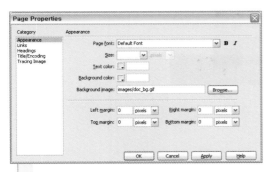

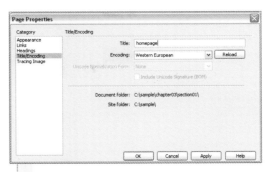

2　Click the [Page Properties] button in the Properties Inspector to open the Page Properties dialog box. Click [Browse]. The Select Image Source dialog box appears. Select the image/doc_bg.gif file from your local site. Click [OK]. This inserts the file as a background image and returns to the Page Properties dialog box. In the Page Properties dialog box, set Left, Right, Top, and Bottom margins to 0 pixels.

3　Select Title/Encoding under Category and enter a name for the page in the Title field.

&lt;&lt; tip

## Page Properties Shortcut

You can also press [Ctrl]-[J] to open the Page Properties dialog box.

4　Now you'll need to insert a masthead above the table, but as you can see here, the table starts right at the top of the page. You will need to insert some empty space above the table. First, select the table.

| Section | 2001 | 2002 | 2003 |
|---|---|---|---|
| Production | 66,437,720 | 56,396,909 | 78,013,259 |
| Inventory | 35,242,223 | 54,433,482 | 75,442,133 |
| Statements | 372,497 | 1,552,427 | 2,575,116 |
| Capital | 45,244,358 | 58,314,368 | 72,688,421 |
| Share | 25,975,652 | 41,352,526 | 17,159,070 |
| Employees | 19,268,706 | 17,193,842 | 12,559,351 |
| Sub Total | 121,822,078 | 114,913,277 | 130,701,670 |
| Sales | 47,255,477 | 33,526,134 | 52,755,185 |
| Credit | 786,465 | 23,305,315 | 22,635,271 |
| Total | 121,822,078 | 113,913,277 | 140,501,670 |

5　Press the left arrow key on the keyboard. This will place the cursor on the left of the table.

6　Now, hit the [Enter] key three times. In the Design View, you will see some extra room above the table. In the Code View, you will see the <P>···</P> tags added.

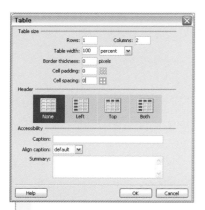

7   In the Design View, click on the second line from the top of the page. Then click on the [Insert Table] icon (▦) in the Insert bar to make a 1 row, 2 columns table. Set the Table Width to 100% and the Cell padding, Cell spacing, and Border thickness to 0. Click OK.

8   Click and drag the main.gif image from the Site panel to the left cell. With the left cell selected, set its width to 750 in the Properties Inspector.

9   Click on the <table> tag at the Tag Selector to select the table. In the Properties Inspector, drag the [Point to File] icon (⊙) next to the Bg Image text field to the table_bg.gif file in the Site panel. If you preview the page in a browser, you will see that the background image will stretch to fill out your browser window's width.

<< note

## The [Delete] and [Backspace] Keys

In this example, an empty line was deliberately left at the top of the page to illustrate the difference between the [Delete] and [Backspace] keys. Click on the top-left corner of the Document window. If you try removing the empty line by pressing the [Delete] key, you will notice that nothing happens. If you use the [Backspace] key, however, you can delete the redundant line.

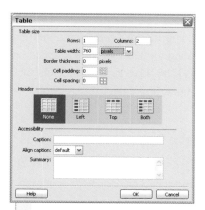

10 Place the cursor below the image and click the [Insert Table] icon (▦) in the Insert bar to create a 1-row, 2-column table with a width of 760 pixels.

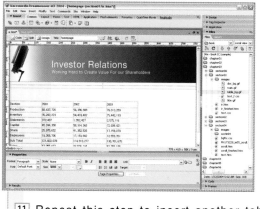

11 Repeat this step to insert another table of the same dimensions. You will be inserting the heading **Company IR Report** into the first table, and embedding the table containing the text and figures into the second table.

12 Now, let's adjust the width of the left cells in both tables. Select the left cell of the first table and set its width to 180 in the Properties Inspector.

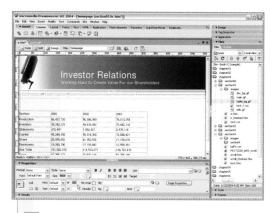

13 Repeat this step on the second table, but set the width to 200 instead.

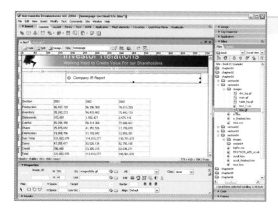

14 Drag the title.gif file from the File panel to the right cell of the first table.

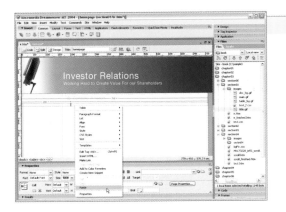

15 Let's embed the table containing the text and figures into the second table in this step. Embedding the table will give it space on the left. Select the table and press [Ctrl]-[X] to cut it. Then, right-click on the right cell of the second table and select [Paste] from the shortcut menu to insert the data.

<< note

## Automatically Defining the Background Image as an Internal Style

With Dreamweaver MX 2004, when a background image is applied, it will automatically be defined as an internal style.

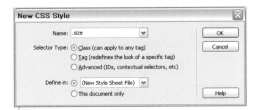

16 Now, let's create the style sheet for aligning the data. First, create a new style sheet by clicking on the [New CSS Style] icon ( ) in the CSS Styles panel. Type in **.size** in the Name field and select [New Style Sheet File] from the [Define In] drop-down menu, as shown here. Click [OK].

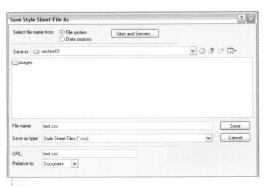

17 When the Save Style Sheet File As dialog box appears, browse to your local site and name the file **text.**

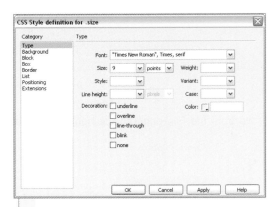

18 The CSS Style Definition dialog box will appear. Check that [Type] is selected in the Category list on the left. Next, select the font and size shown here and click [OK].

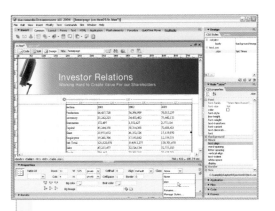

19 Select the table. Then click on [Size] in the CSS Styles panel to change the font and font size of all the text in one go.

86

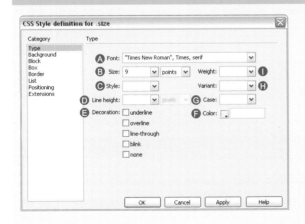

**20** To right-align the text, go to the Rule panel and set the text-align option under the Block category to Right. Note that this time saving function is not available in older versions of Dreamweaver.

**21** Let's add a small space between the table and the text. In order to add this as a new style, go to the CSS Styles panel and click on the [New CSS Style] icon ( ). Type in **.rightPadd** in the Name field and click [OK].

<< tip

# The Type Category

**⊙ Style**: Choose from normal, italic, and oblique styles.

**⊙ Line height**: Determines the spacing between lines. You can select Normal to have this calculated automatically, or enter an exact value.

**⊙ Decoration**: Lets you underline, overline*, or add a line through the text. You can also choose to make the text blink*. For text, the default setting is None. If you set Decoration to None for a link, you will remove the underline from it.

**⊙ Color**: Used to determine text color.

**⊙ Case**: Choose Capitalize, UPPERCASE, or lowercase.

**⊙ Variant**: Choose from normal and small-caps.

**⊙ Weight**: Specifies text thickness in absolute and relative terms. Choose from lighter to bolder or from values ranging from 100 to 900. As a guide, normal is equivalent to 400 while bold is equivalent to 700.

**⊙ Font**: Select from a list of preset font combinations, or create your own.

**⊙ Size**: You can set an absolute size or relative size for your text, depending on how you choose the size and the unit of measurement. Choose a specific font size from 9 to 36 or a relative font size from xx-small to xx-large.

*\* For these options, Dreamweaver does not show you the actual effect after applying it in the Document window.*

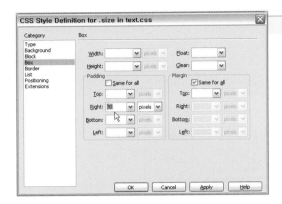

22 When the CSS Style Definition dialog box appears, select Box from the Category list on the left. Uncheck the [Same for all] option under Padding and set the Right padding value to 30 pixels. Click [OK].

23 You can see that the rightPadd style has been added to the CSS Styles panel.

24 Select the left column. Right-click on the rightPadd style in the CSS Styles panel and select [Apply] from the shortcut menu. Note that a space of 30 pixels is now inserted to the right of the text in the cells.

<< tip

## The Block Category

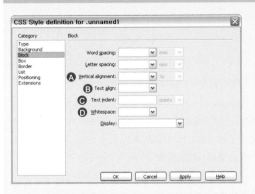

Ⓐ *Vertical Alignment: Used to determine vertical alignment.

Ⓑ Text Align: Used to determine text alignment—left, center, right, or justify.

Ⓒ *Text Indent: Determines how much the first line of a block of text indents.

Ⓓ *Whitespace: Lets you choose how to use the empty space within a selection. Select normal to ignore extra white space, pre to preserve the original white space setting, or nowrap to allow the line to break only when a <br> tag is encountered.

* For these options, Dreamweaver does not show you the actual effect after applying it in the Document window.

25 Repeat this step for the other columns.

26 Select the first row in the table and, in the Properties Inspector, click on the [Color Box] icon (▣) next to Bg to select the #CCCCCC background color—or any other color you like.

<< note

## Selecting Several Cells at the Same Time

You use the [Ctrl] key when selecting several cells at the same time. Holding down the [Ctrl] key, you can click on each of the cells in turn. Alternatively, when selecting blocks of adjacent cells, like in this example, click when the arrow icon appears around the top row's border and then drag downwards to include the other cells in the table.

27 Select the rows from Production to Credit. In the Properties Inspector, click on the text field beside the [Color Box] icon (▣) and type in #E2E9E9 to set it as the background color. You can choose whatever color you want but from a design perspective, it is better to use different shades of the same color or colors that are similar. Using completely different colors will make the table too confusing. When professionals design commercial Web sites, everything, right down to the color of the tables, is determined beforehand and strictly followed.

<< note

## Choosing a Color

In Dreamweaver and other graphics applications, you can choose a color by entering its hexadecimal value (#000000, for example, represents black), typing in a name (black, for example), or by picking the color from the color palette.

<< tip

## Using More than 216 Colors

The color palette in Dreamweaver is a Web-safe color palette. Web-safe colors are colors that appear the same in Netscape Navigator and Microsoft Internet Explorer on both Windows and Macintosh systems.

To select a color outside this palette, click on the color box in the Properties Inspector. Then click on the [System Color Picker] button (▣) in the palette. Select a color, and click [Add to Custom Colors] to save this color for future use.

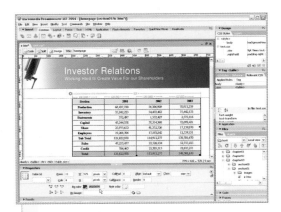

**28** Select the cells at the top and on the left and click on the [Bold] ( **B** ) and [Align Center] icons ( ≡ ), as shown here. Select the last row and fill it with the #9999FF background color.

**29** With the entire table selected, set the background color to #000099. This color is much darker than the background colors you have set so far. Because the CellPad value is set to 1, this color will show through the gap between the cells, creating a border.

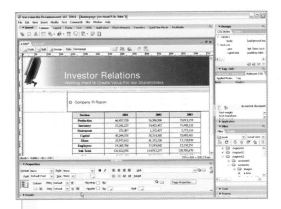

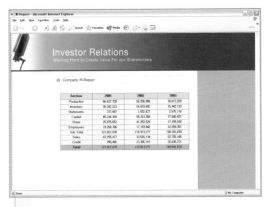

**30** You can see that the header, Company IR Report, and the table are too close together. Select the table containing the header and set its height to 80 pixels to create more room between the two tables.

**31** Press [F12] to preview your work in the Web browser.

# Creating Employee Profile Pages

In this section, you will create a set of employee profile pages by using tables and style sheets. You will explore the box and background options for defining style sheets while also learning to create a rollover menu with links. Additionally, you will learn to work in the Layout View, and by the end of this exercise, understand the difference between Layout View and Standard View.

**Final Files**

\Sample\Chapter03\Section02\finished\profile_1.htm, profile_2.htm, profile_3.htm, profile_4.htm

<< note

## Resource Files

Remember to copy the resource files on the CD-ROM to your local site before you start each exercise in this book.

[1] In the File panel, select your site folder and right-click. Select [New File] from the shortcut menu. Name the new file **profile_1.htm**. Repeat the step to create another three files, naming them **profile_2.htm**, **profile_3.htm**, **profile_4.htm**.

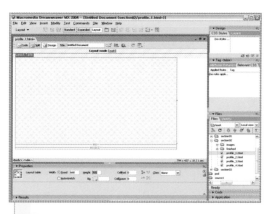

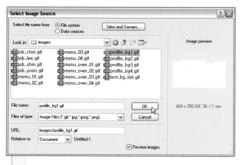

2 Now, let's start off by creating a profile page for the CEO of this company. Open profile_1.htm. In the Insert bar, pull down the menu on the left corner. Select [Layout]. Next, click on the [Layout Mode] button ( Layout ) to convert to Layout View. Make sure your cursor is in the Design View window before you perform this step or you won't be able to choose Layout View.

3 Click on the [Draw Layout Table] button ( ) and then drag to create the table, as shown here. In the Properties Inspector, set the table width to 660 and the height to 360 so that the table will be able to accommodate the background image you will be inserting in the following step.

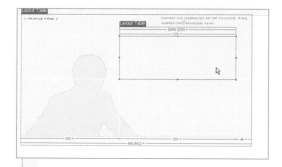

4 In order to insert the background image, click on the [Standard Mode] button ( Standard ) to go back to Standard View. In the Properties Inspector, click on the expander arrow in the lower-right corner to display all the properties of the table. Click on the [Browse for File] icon ( ) next to Bg Image and choose the profile_bg1.gif image from the image folder in your local site.

5 You will now insert an image of some text describing the CEO's position. Click the [Layout Mode] button ( Layout ) and then click the [Draw Layout Table] icon ( ). Drag on the table to insert a new table, as shown.

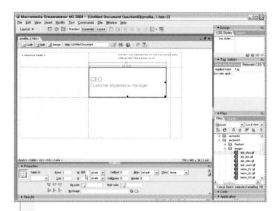

6 Go back to Standard View. Then select and insert the job_choi.gif image file from the File panel. If the image is larger than the table, the table will adjust to accommodate the image size. If the table is taller than the image, the image may tile and you will see the word CEO repeated at the bottom. To hide it, simply drag the border of the table to shorten it.

7 Click on the [Draw Layout Cell] button (▦). Drag below the CEO table to insert a new cell, as shown here. Repeat the step to insert another cell at the bottom. Click on a cell and type in some information about the CEO. Repeat the step in the other cell to complete the profile. Remember to use the [Shift]-[Enter] keys to insert a line break when typing in the next line, hitting [Enter] only will create too much vertical space between the lines.

8 You will now add a rollover image at the bottom of the page. This image will be used as a menu that will link visitors to the profiles of other employees. In the Insert bar, click on the [Standard Mode] button. Next, switch to the [Common] Insert Bar and click on the [Images] button (▣). Select the [Rollover Image] option (▣ Rollover Image).

<< note

## Creating Type Effects

Although you can type any information directly onto the page, you can create more interesting type effects by using another graphics program, such as Photoshop. You can save your Photoshop text as an image file for use in Dreamweaver.

<< note

## Moving Layout Tables Around

It's easy to move layout tables in Layout View. Just select the table border or the [Layout Table] tab and drag the table to the new location. On the other hand, moving tables in Standard View is tricky because the table doesn't move as one and the borders have to be adjusted one by one.

<< note

## The Difference Between Layout Tables and Layout Cells

In Layout View, you can insert layout cells into a layout table, but you cannot insert layout tables into layout cells. Therefore, insert a layout table if you need to divide it further and insert a layout cell if no further divisions will be made. In Standard View, however, you can insert a table into a cell and vice versa.

**9** In the Insert Rollover Image dialog box, click on the [Browse] button next to the Original Image text field. Select the menu_01.gif image from your local site and click [OK]. In the same way, select the menu_over_01.gif image as the rollover image.

&lt;&lt; note

## Rollover Images

On some Web pages, when you place your cursor over an image, another image appears. This other image that appears is called a rollover image. Rollover images are fun, and using them helps visitors make sure that they are making the correct selection. When creating rollover images, you need two images of the same size. If the images are of different sizes, the rollover effect will appear disjointed.

**10** In the [When Clicked, Go To URL] text field, enter **profile_1.htm**. This means that when a visitor clicks on the image, he will be brought to the profile_1.htm page. Click [OK].

**11** In the same way, create the rollover images that will take us to the profile pages of the other employees. Use the images and links below.

| Original Image | Rollover Image | URL |
| --- | --- | --- |
| menu_01.gif | menu_over_01.gif | profile_1.htm |
| menu_02.gif | menu_over_02.gif | profile_2.htm |
| menu_03.gif | menu_over_03.gif | profile_3.htm |
| menu_04.gif | menu_over_04.gif | profile_4.htm |

&lt;&lt; note

## Naming Files

In the preceding step, it was easy for you to match the original image files with the rollover image files because the files were named systematically. I would recommend that you use a logical and easy-to-understand system when naming files. In this way, you will not have to waste time looking for the right file, especially when you are building a large Web site.

&lt;&lt; note

**Table Groups**

Try to organize all the text and images on a page inside a table or a few tables. This will group all these elements together, making it easy to edit or modify them at the same time.

12 In the Insert bar, click on the [Insert Table] icon (▦) to make a 1-row, 1-column, 660-pixel table. Click [OK]. Select all the rollover images, as shown here, and move them inside the table.

13 You now have two tables on the page; the main table containing the CEO profile and the table containing the menu. Select each of the tables and set Align to the Center in the Properties Inspector. The CellPad, CellSpace, and Border Thickness of both tables should be set to 0. Also, remove any space between the two tables using the [Backspace] key.

14 You are now ready to use style sheets to format the tables. In the CSS Style panel, click on the [New CSS Style] icon (🔲) and name the style sheet **.nameText**. Select [New Style Sheet File] under Define In to designate this file as an external style sheet. It is important to do this because you will be applying the style to several different pages.

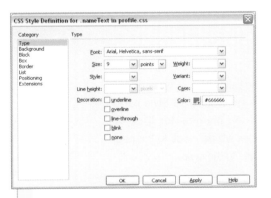

15 When the Save Style Sheet File As dialog box appears, enter the style name **profile.css**. Click [Save].

16 In the CSS Style Definition dialog box, set the font, size, and color as shown here and click [OK].

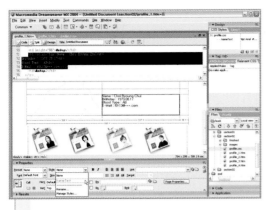

**17** [Ctrl]-[click] to select the cell as shown, then select the nameText style from the Properties Inspector to apply the designated font, size, and color.

**18** You will now edit the style in order to add cell padding. In the Relevant CSS Style panel, enter the left and top margins for [Box] as shown here. Changes will be made to the page as you make changes to the style.

&lt;&lt; note

## CSS Style Names

When naming CSS Styles, you cannot use symbols such as _ or - to split words, making it difficult to make out long names. But you can try capitalizing words instead. For example, it is much easier to read **.nameText** than it is to read **.nametext**.

&lt;&lt; note

## The Box Category

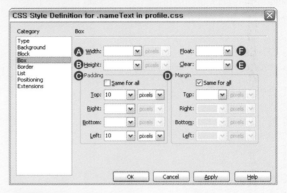

**Ⓐ Width**: Sets box width.

**Ⓑ Height**: Sets box height.

**Ⓒ Padding**: Specifies the spacing inside the box.

**Ⓓ Margin**: Specifies the space between the border and another element.

**Ⓔ Clear**: Sets the sides that do not allow layers. Choose from Left, Right, Both, or None.

**Ⓕ Float**: Choose from Left, Right, or None to determine on which side other elements such as text and images will float around the box.

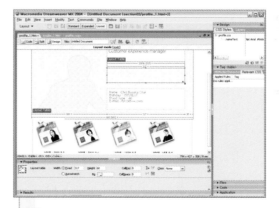

**19** Switch to Layout Mode. Select the middle cell, as shown, and press [Delete]. Click on the [Layout Table] icon (▣) to create a new table of the same size in place of the deleted cell.

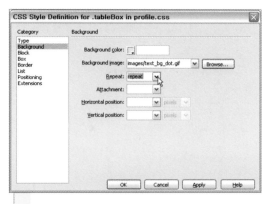

**20** Let's create a background style for the new table. Click on the [New CSS Style] icon (⊞) in the CSS Styles panel. Name the style **.tableBox** and define it in profile.css. Click [OK].

**21** Select the Background category and click on the [Browse] button next to the Background Image text field. Select the text_bg_dot.gif file from your local site. Click [OK]. Then select Repeat so that the image tiles in the background. Click [OK].

**<< note**

## The Background Category

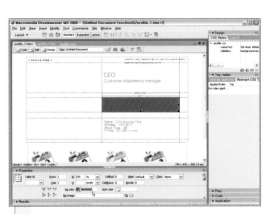

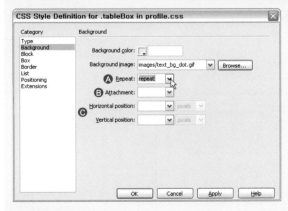

**22** Switch to Standard View and select the <table> tag from the Tag Selector and set the Bg color to gray (#999999).

**Ⓐ Repeat**: Choose from no-repeat, repeat, repeat-x, and repeat-y to determine whether and how the background repeats. Choose Repeat-x to repeat the image along the x-axis or Repeat-y to repeat along the y-axis.

**Ⓑ Attachment**: Choose either to fix the image at its original position or to scroll with the page. This feature is not supported in Netscape Navigator.

**Ⓒ Horizontal Position and Vertical Position**: Use these options to specify the location of the image in relation to the element (for example, position in a table). If Attachment is set to Fixed, the position is relative to the Document window and not to the element. This feature is not supported in Netscape Navigator.

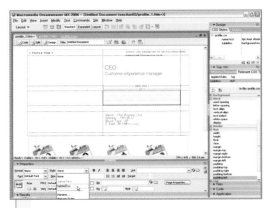

**23** Click inside the table to make sure the table is no longer selected. Select <td> from the Tag Selector to select the cell. Make sure you select the correct tag. In the Properties Inspector, select the .tableBox style to apply the background style. The background image is actually much smaller than the table, but because you selected the Repeat option, it repeats to fill the entire table.

**24** In the Properties Inspector, set the vertical alignment to Top. Enter a few lines of text. Move to the next line of text by pressing [Shift]-[Enter]. Simply pressing [Enter] will create paragraph stops. Looking at the text you have entered, you may notice that the text does not line up exactly with the lines in the background image.

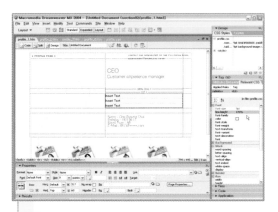

**25** In the Tag Inspector, set the line height to 170% and the font size to 9 points under the Font category. The default Line Height is 100% but by setting it to 170%, you are increasing the spacing between the lines of text. Experiment with the settings until you get the text to sit on the lines in the background. When you are done, press [Ctrl]-[S] to save your work. You have now completed the first file.

**26** In step 1, you created the blank profile pages, profile_2.htm, profile_3.htm and profile_4.htm, so that you can insert the links into the rollover menu on profile_1.htm. In the following steps, you will replace these blank profile pages with the profile_1.htm file, since the format for all these pages is the same. Select [File] - [Save As] from the menu bar. Name the file **profile_2.htm**. Since the file already exists, a warning message will appear asking if you wish to overwrite the existing file. Click [Yes].

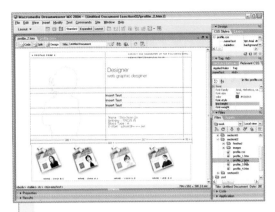

27 In profile_2.htm, change the background image to profile_bg2.gif, the job title to job_shin.gif, and replace the text in the profile section. The rollover menu is the same on all the profile pages so let's leave it as it is. Click [File] - [Save]. Repeat the steps on profile_3.htm (Yoon's profile) and profile_4.htm (Lee's profile).

28 Preview your work in the Web browser. Check that the links in the rollover menu work properly.

# Exercise 3

# Creating Rollover Effects in Tables

Rollover effects are especially useful on busy Web pages with many lines of text, as they provide visual cues on interactivity. In this section, you will learn how to add a rollover effect to a table by editing its tags directly. This technique is often used for creating forums and bulletin boards.

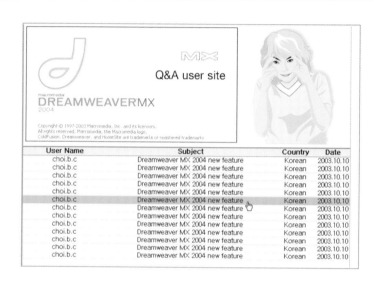

**Start File**

\Sample\Chapter03\Section03\table_over.htm

**Final File**

\Sample\Chapter03\Section03\table_over_finished.htm

<< note

## Resource Files

Remember to copy the resource files on the CD-ROM to your local site before you start each exercise in this book.

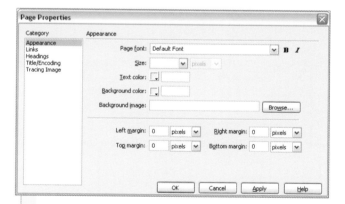

1 Open table_over.htm and select [Modify] - [Page Properties]. Click the [Browse] button next to the Background Image field.

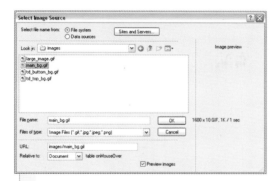

2　The Select Image Source dialog box appears. Select main_bg.gif from the local folder. In the Image Preview window, you will see that main_bg.gif is a long thin strip of 1600 pixels by 10 pixels. The height only needs to be 10 pixels because background images are tiled repeatedly so they cover the entire page. Click [OK].

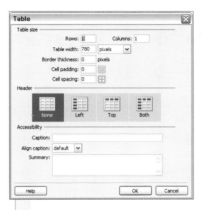

3　When the Page Properties dialog box appears, click [OK].

4　Click the [Table] icon (  ) of the [Common] menu in the Insert bar to create a table. In the Table dialog box, set both Rows and Columns to 1. Set Table Width to 780 pixels. Border thickness, Cell padding, and Cell spacing should all be set to 0. Click [OK].

5　Drag large_image.gif from the Files panel into the table.

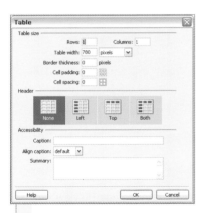

6 Place the insertion point below the first table and click the [Table] icon (⊞) of the [Common] menu in the Insert bar to create another table. In the Table dialog box, set both Rows and Columns to 1. Set Table Width to 780 pixels. Click [OK].

7 In the Properties Inspector, set H to 22 pixels and drag the [Point to File] icon for the Bg Image field to td_top_bg.gif in the Files panel. You should be able to see a sky blue background image in the table.

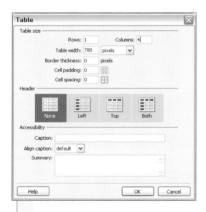

8 Click inside the table created in step 7 and click the [Table] icon (⊞) of the [Common] menu in the Insert bar to create another table. In the Table dialog box, set with Rows to 1 and Columns to 4. Set Table Width to 780 pixels. Click [OK].

9 Type **User Name**, **Subject**, **Country**, and **Date** into the cells in sequence. Select the four cells. In the Properties Inspector, click the [Bold] icon (**B**) and the [Align Center] icon (≣) to boldface and center the text.

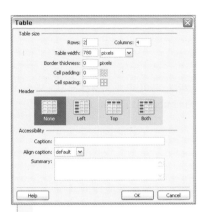

10 Place the insertion point below the bottom table and click the [Table] icon (🔲) of the [Common] menu in the Insert bar to create another table. In the Table dialog box, set with Rows to 2 and Columns to 4. Set Table Width to 780 pixels. Click [OK].

11 Move the cursor to the lower row of the table and click the <tr> tag and, in the Properties Inspector, click the [Merge] icon (🔲) to merge the four cells of the lower row into one.

12 Drag td_buttom_bg.gif from the Files panel into the merged cell. Note that the size of the inserted image is 10 x 10 pixels and the image is composed of just one color.

13 Select the image. In the Properties Inspector, change W to 780 and H to 1.

14 Then, click the [Resample] icon (🔲) to change the image size. When the warning message appears, click [OK].

| | | | | |
|---|---|---|---|---|
| Image Path | C:\Sample\Chapter03\Section03\images\td_button_bg.gif | | | |

**15** The bottom row of the table is now 780 pixels wide and 1 pixel high. This is not very clear in Edit Mode. To view it better, click the [Layout] tab of the Insert bar and click the [Expanded] button ( Expanded ) to change to Expanded View.

**16** Right-click the <tr> tag in the Tag Selector to select the cell at the top and bring up the contextual menu. Select [Edit Tag].

**17** Change the selected tag to <tr onMouseover="this.style. backgroundColor='#99CCCC'" style="CURSOR: hand" onMouseout = "this.style.backgroundColor = '#f5f5f5'">.

**18** This new tag sets the background color of the table to #F5F5F5. It also specifies that the table color be changed to #99CCCC when the mouse moves over it.

**104**

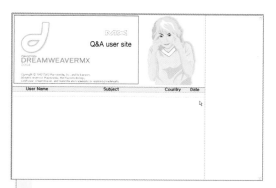

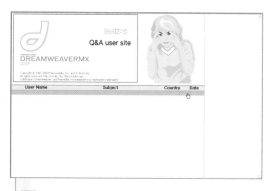

19 Press [F12] to preview your work in the Web browser.

20 Observe how the color changes down the table.

21 Select and make a copy of the table at the bottom.

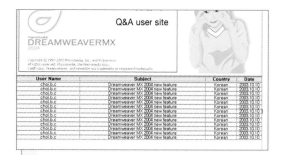

22 Select the entire table, then click [Edit] - [Copy] to make a copy of the table. Then, click on [Edit] - [Paste] several times to make repeated copies of the table. In dynamic applications such as forums, the <tr> tags are created automatically, but for this beginner's exercise, you will perform a manual copy-and-paste instead.

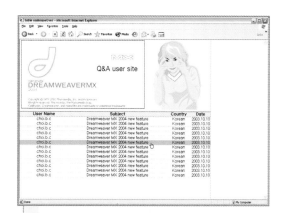

23 Press [F12] to preview the page in the Web browser. Note the rollover effect for the tables.

# Creating Unique Scrollbars

When the contents of a Web page cannot fit on one page, a scrollbar will appear automatically. In this section, you will learn how to customize the color of the scrollbars using an extension. The colored scrollbar feature is supported in Internet Explorer version 5.5 and later

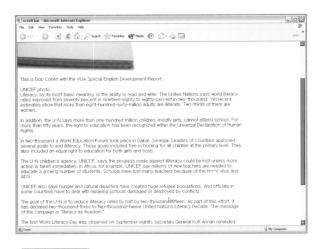

**Start File**

\Sample\Chapter03\Section04\scroll.htm

**Final File**

\Sample\Chapter03\Section04\scroll_finished.htm

**Extension File**

MX173228_ie55_scroll.mxp

<< note

### Resource Files

Remember to copy the resource files on the CD-ROM to your local site before you start each exercise in this book.

Download the extension file from the Macromedia Web site. See page 9 for instructions for downloading extensions.

1 Double-click the extension file to open the Macromedia Extension Manager program.

**2** After installing the extension, restart Dreamweaver to activate the changes.

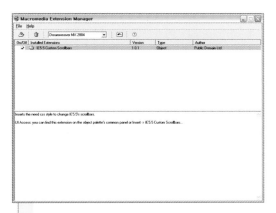

**3** Close the Macromedia Extension Manager program.

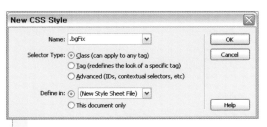

**4** Open scroll.htm and click the [New CSS Style] icon (⊞) in the CSS Styles panel. The New CSS Style dialog box appears. Type **.bgFix** in the Name field. Under the Define In options, select [New Style Sheet File] to create an external style sheet. Click [OK].

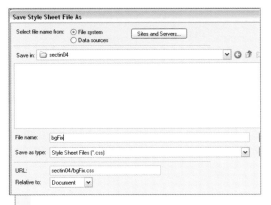

**5** The Save Style Sheet File As dialog box appears. Navigate to the local site and type **bgFix.css** as the file name. Click [OK].

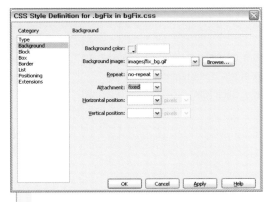

**6** The CSS Style Definition dialog box appears. Select Background from the Category list. Click the [Browse] icon and select fix_bg.gif from the local folder. Set Repeat to no-repeat and Attachment to fixed. This defines the background image as a style sheet and creates a fixed background, regardless of how much content there is on the Web page. Click [OK].

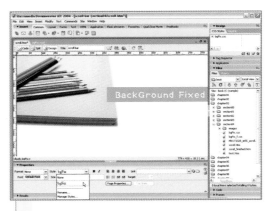

**7** Select the <body> tag in the Tag Selector. In the Properties Inspector, set Style to bgFix. This applies the background image defined earlier.

**8** To add color to the scrollbar, click the [IE 5.5 Custom Scrollbars] icon (▤) in the [Common] menu in the Insert Bar.

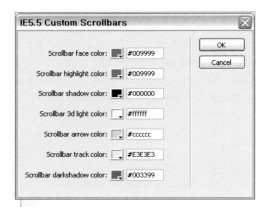

**9** When the IE5.5 Custom Scrollbars dialog box appears, type in the hexadecimal value for the colors as shown. Click [OK].

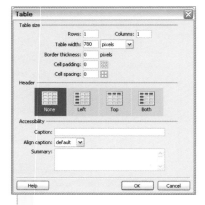

**10** To check if color has been added to the scrollbar, and to see if the background remains fixed, you need to create content that runs for more than one page. Click the [Table] icon (▦) of the [Common] menu in the Insert bar to create a table. In the Table dialog box, set both Rows and Columns to 1. Set Table Width to 780 pixels and click [OK].

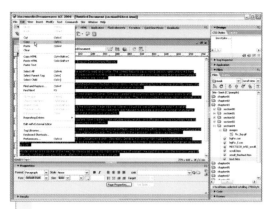

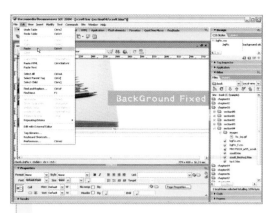

11 Open text.htm on the local folder and select [Edit] - [Select All and [Edit] - [Copy] to select and copy the entire text.

12 Return to scroll.htm and place the cursor within the table created in step 7. Click [Edit] - [Paste] to paste the text.

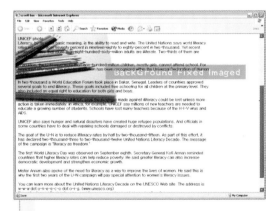

13 Press [F12] to preview your work in the Web browser. Note that color has been added to the scrollbar.

14 Also note that when you scroll down the page, the background image remains fixed. Style sheets make it easy to fix the background image on pages that require the background image to remain in place.

If you don't want the background image to remain fixed, you can change this quite easily in the Tag Inspector.

❶ Click the CSS Styles panel and click .bgFix.

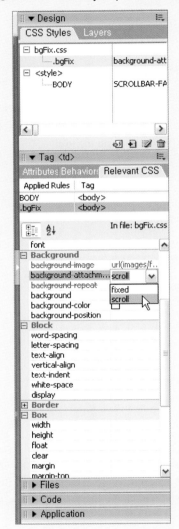

❷ In the Relevant CSS panel, change the Background Attachment property from fixed to scroll.

❸ Now the background image moves with the scrollbar.

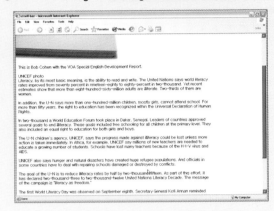

<< note

## Scrollbar Colors

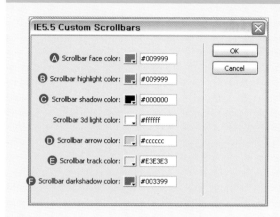

**A** **Scrollbar face color**: Color of the scrollbar.

**B** **Scrollbar highlight color**: Color of highlighted edges at the left and top of the scrollbar.

**C** **Scrollbar shadow color**: Color of shadow at right and bottom of the scrollbar.

**D** **Scrollbar arrow color**: Color of top and bottom scrollbar arrows.

**E** **Scrollbar track color**: Scrollbar background color.

**F** **Scrollbar clarkshadow color**: Color of outline at the right and bottom edges of the scrollbar.

Chapter | 4

# Using Frames

Frames are most commonly used to create fixed elements such as a navigation bar. When you explore a huge Web site that has many pages, it is not easy to remember exactly what you have already visited, where specific items are located, or even where your current location is relative to the entire Web site. In this chapter, you will learn to use frames to make your site more organized and easier to navigate.

# Introduction to Frames

Frames give your Web page great versatility by creating separate functional elements such as a navigation menu or content windows. The rule, however, is to keep the design simple. Having too many frames can confuse the user and can be difficult to debug.

## About Frames

Frames allow the browser window to be divided into two or more areas, each holding a different HTML document. This page-within-a-page device typically allows the user to view and scroll through content in the main frames while being able to access links and other information in ancillary frames.

## Basic Frames Terminology

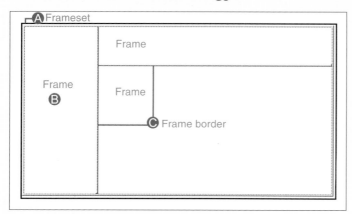

🅐 **Frameset**: A frameset is a set of frames defined in a frameset definition document. In the illustration, the three frames belong to a frameset.

🅑 **Frame**: A frame is like a window within a window, with each frame having its own contents, design, and scrollbar.

🅒 **Frame border**: This is the divider between two frames.

**Frameset Definition Document**: Also known as a frameset page, a frameset definition document is the HTML document that defines the layout and properties of a set of frames. This document tells the Web browser how to display the frames.

## The Frames Panel

The Frames panel provides an easy overview of a frameset and is useful for selecting and modifying frames. The shortcut keys for accessing the panel are [Shift]-[F2]. You can also select [Window] - [Frames] from the main menu bar.

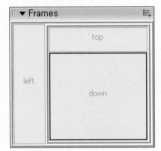

## Creating Frames

There are a number of ways to create frames. Let's look at each of these methods:

## Using the Insert Bar

Of all the methods for inserting frames, using the Insert bar is probably the easiest because it provides a visual cue. In the Insert bar, the names of the frameset commands are set beside icons showing what the framesets look like. To insert a frame using the Insert bar, click the [Frames] button ( ▣▾ ) in the [Layout] menu of the Insert bar to pull down a list of 13 predefined framesets. Select and click an icon to apply a frameset.

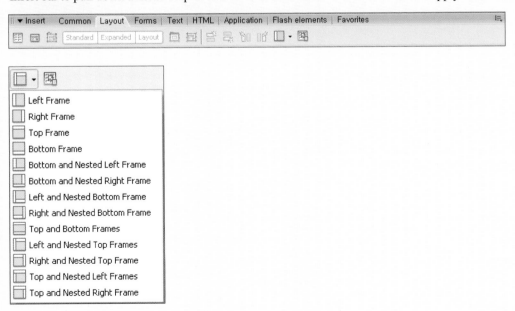

## Using the Insert Menu

Another way of inserting frames is to use the Insert menu on the menu bar. To use the Insert menu, click [Insert] - [HTML] - [Frames] from the menu bar and then select a frameset.

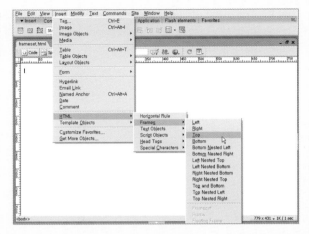

## Using the Modify Menu

To create your own frame layout, click [Modify] - [Frameset] and choose to split the page left, right, up, or down. When the frame border appears, you can drag it to a new position. Each frame can then be split further by using the [Modify] - [Frameset] command.

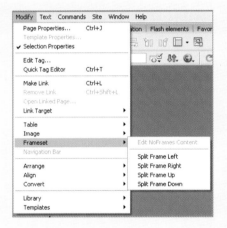

## Dragging a Frame Border

A more flexible way of creating frames is to drag frame borders from the side of the page.

1. From the menu bar, select [View] - [Visual Aids] - [Frame Borders] to activate the default frame border around the page.

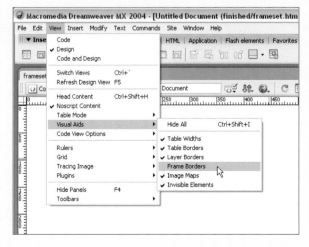

2. To create a frame, place the mouse over a side of the page and drag the frame border to a new position.

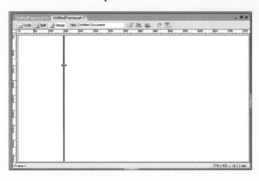
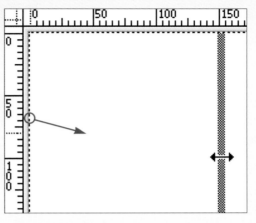

## Using the [Alt] and [Ctrl] Keys to Divide Frames

**[Alt]-[Drag]:** Using [Alt]-[drag] on frame borders inside a page lets you split frames further by dragging out a new frame border. Dragging the frame borders inside a page without holding the [Alt] key will only move the frame borders without splitting the frames.

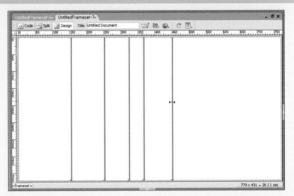

**[Ctrl]-[Drag]:** To create a new frame without cutting across all the frames in its path, hold down [Crtl] when dragging to push the existing frame onto the page.

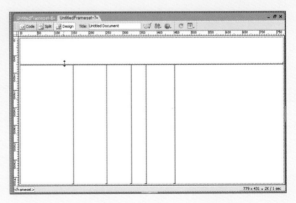

## Deleting Frames

To delete a frame, drag the frame border off the page or to the border of the parent frame. Note that if you have inserted content into the frame, Dreamweaver will prompt you to save the document first.

## Saving Frames

When working with frames, you have to save frames individually and as a frameset.

1. Open a new document and enter some text. Click the [Frames] button (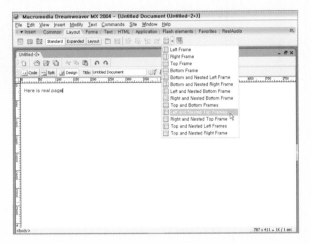) in the [Layout] menu of the Insert bar to pull down a list of predefined frame designs. Select and click Left and Nested Top Frames.

2. Select [File] - [Save Frame] from the menu bar. Save the file as **main.htm**.

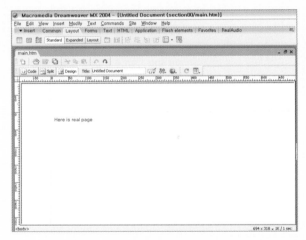

3. Click in the top frame and type in **top**. Select [File] - [Save Frame] from the menu bar and save the frame as **top.htm**. Similarly, type in **left** in the left frame and save it as **left.htm**.

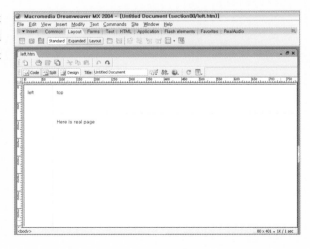

&lt;&lt; tip

## Unsaved Frames

On the tab at the top of the Document window, you will see the file name of a frame. Every frame must have a name so that you can set up links for it. If the frame has not been saved, Dreamweaver gives it a temporary file name. Once you save the frame, the name will change to the one you have specified.

4. In the Frames panel, click on the frame border surrounding all the frames. Then select [File] - [Save Frameset] from the menu bar.

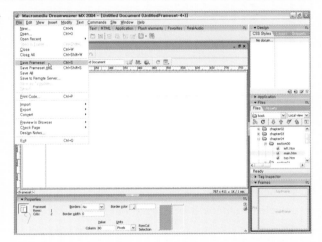

5. In the Save Frameset dialog box, enter **frameset.htm** as the file name.

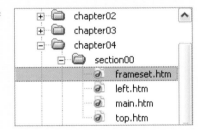

&lt;&lt; tip

## Changing Frame Names

To change the name of a frame, select the frame in the Frames panel and enter a new name in the Src field of the Properties Inspector.

You can specify the size of a frame in pixels or as a percentage. This attribute can easily be changed using the Properties Inspector.

1. Create a new file, **frame_size.htm**. Click the [Frames] button (⊞▾) in the [Layout] menu of the Insert bar to pull down a list of predefined frame designs. Select Left Frame. Select the frameset in the Frames panel.

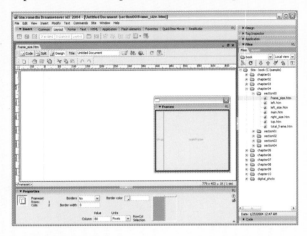

2. In the Properties Inspector, select the left frame in the RowCol Selection visual representation. The selected frame will be grayed out in a darker shade in the RowCol Selection visual. Set Column to 150 pixels.

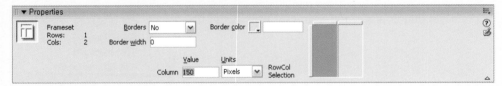

3. The right frame will automatically be set to 1 Relative. This means the browser will always have the left frame at 150 pixels, while the right frame will vary depending on the screen size.

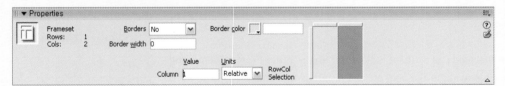

<< tip

**Frame Size in Percentage**

In the above example, if you had set both frames to size as a percentage, each frame would be sized as a ratio of the width of the user's browser window.

# Frameset Properties Inspector

You can use the Properties Inspector to view and edit most frame and frameset properties.

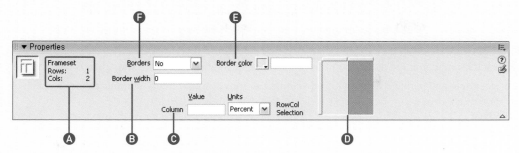

Ⓐ **Frameset**: Indicates the number of rows and columns in the frameset.

Ⓑ **Border width**: Specifies the border thickness.

Ⓒ **Column**: Specifies the frame size in pixels, as a percentage, or as a relative value.

Ⓓ **RowCol Selection**: Provides visual tools for frame selection. The selected frame is darkened.

Ⓔ **Border color**: Determines the color of the border.

Ⓕ **Borders**: The border does not appear if this is set to No. The border appears if this is set to Yes and Border width is greater than 0.

# Frame Properties Inspector

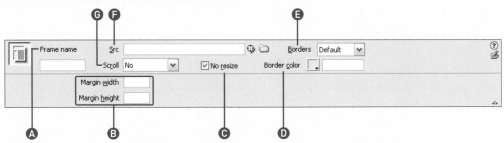

Ⓐ **Frame name**: Specifies the name of the frame.

Ⓑ **Margin width/height**: Set these to 0 if you want to remove any space between the frames so they appear seamlessly joined to one another.

Ⓒ **No resize**: Check this option if you do not want the frames to be resizable in the browser window.

Ⓓ **Border color**: Determines the color of the border.

Ⓔ **Borders**: Disables the border when set to No and enables the border if set to Yes. If set to Default, the browser will determine how the border is displayed.

Ⓕ **Src**: Specifies the source or the name of the frame document.

Ⓖ **Scroll**: When set to No, no scrollbars will appear around the frame. If set to yes, scrollbars will appear around the frame. When set to Auto, the scrollbars appear only when the contents of the frame will not fit in the browser window. If Default is selected, the scrollbars appear depending on the browser's default setting.

A Web site is like a building. Just as a building has a front door and many rooms on each floor, a Web site has a home page and a navigation bar with elements or icons pointing you to many other associated Web pages. If the Web site is well designed, the interface will indicate clearly how the entire Web site is structured so you know exactly where you are at any point in time. When designing your Web site, always try to make the navigation as simple and painless as possible so visitors can move around freely without getting lost.

## Insert Navigation Bar Dialog Box

In Exercise 2, you will learn how to create a navigation bar step by step. Before we go on that, let's look at the settings in the Insert Navigation Bar dialog box.

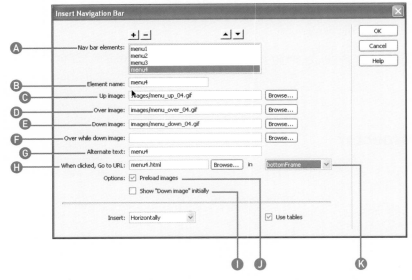

Ⓐ **Nav bar elements**: Displays names of the navigation bar elements already defined.

Ⓑ **Element name**: Specifies a unique name for the navigation bar element.

Ⓒ **Up image**: Specifies the original image for the navigation bar element.

Ⓓ **Over image**: Specifies the image that appears when the cursor moves over the navigation bar element.

Ⓔ **Down image**: Specifies the image that appears when the mouse is held down on the navigation bar element.

Ⓕ **Over while down image**: Specifies the image that appears if the mouse leaves and then enters again–all the while with the mouse button held down.

Ⓖ **Alternate text**: Specifies the text that appears in place of the image in case the image fails to load or the browser is set to text mode.

Ⓗ **When clicked, Go to URL**: Specifies the Web page to jump to when the navigation bar element is clicked.

Ⓘ **Show "Down image" initially**: This sets the initial image to the Down image specified earlier.

**J** **Preload images**: Make sure you check this option so the browser will preload all the images needed for the rollover effect before the rollover item becomes activated.

**K** **In [frame]**: Specifies the target frame.

## Using Inline Frames

Inline frames are often used to display contents in a scrollable (optional) window inside a browser window. Also known as floating frames, inline frames are different from normal frames. While normal frames divide a browser window into subwindows, inline frames appear inside a page in the same way images do on the page. Inline frames scroll with the rest of the document and can be scrolled away.

```
1  <!DOCTYPE HTML PUBLIC "-//W3C//DTD HTML 4.01 Transitional//EN"
2  "http://www.w3.org/TR/html4/loose.dtd">
3  <html>
4  <head>
5  <title>Untitled Document</title>
6  <meta http-equiv="Content-Type" content="text/html; charset=iso-8859-1">
7  </head>
8
9  <body>
10 <table width="600" border="1">
11   <tr>
12     <td><iframe src="http://www.yahoo.com" width="500" height="300" frameborder="0" scrolling="no"></iframe></td>
13   </tr>
14 </table>
15 </body>
16 </html>
```

To create an inline frame, you have to insert the <iframe> tag in the Code window. In Exercise 3, you will learn how to do this, but let's first get familiar with some of the iFrame attributes.

## iFrame Attributes

**src**: Specifies the source document that will appear in the iFrame window.

**name**: Specifies a unique identifier for the iFrame. The iFrame can also be the target for an external document.

**width**: Specifies the frame width in pixels.

**height**: Specifies the frame height in pixels.

**marginwidth**: Specifies the left and right margins of the frame in pixels.

**marginheight**: Specifies the top and bottom margins of the frame in pixels.

**scrolling**: Enables the scrollbars when set to Yes and disables the scrollbars when set to No. If set to Auto, the browser determines how the scrollbars will appear.

**frameborder**: Enables the frame border when set to Yes and disables the frame border when set to No.

**hspace/vspace**: Specifies the horizontal and vertical length of the frame.

**align**: Aligns the iFrame, not the content inside the iFrame.

# 1

# Designing a Link Page Using Frames

Do you have a huge list of favorite Web sites that you wish to share with others? Creating a Web page of recommended links is the easiest way to do that. In this section, you will learn how to use frames to create a really cool-looking Web page of your favorite links.

<< note

## Resource Files

Remember to copy the resource files on the CD-ROM to your local site before you start each exercise in this book.

1 Open menu.htm. Note the rollover image already in the file. Do not insert any <br> or <p> tags in the white space below the table as this will change the page layout.

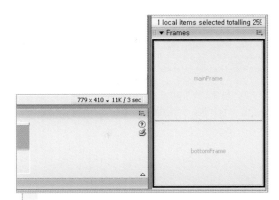

2　Click the [Frames] button (□·) in the [Layout] menu of the Insert bar and select [Bottom Frame] from the pull-down list of predefined framesets.

3　Click on [Window] - [Frames] to bring up the Frames panel. Then click on the border of the frameset to select the frameset.

4　In the Properties Inspector, select the upper frame and set Row Value to 220 pixels. Then select the lower frame and set Row to 1 Relative.

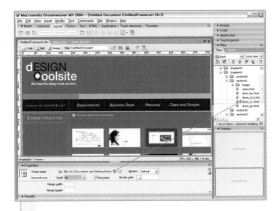

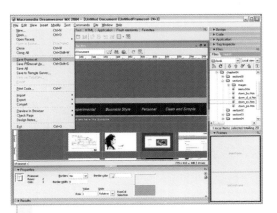

5　In the Frames panel, select the bottomFrame. Then in the Properties Inspector, drag the [Point to File] icon to set Src to down_ex.htm. This loads the document into the lower frame.

6　Select the frameset. Select [File] - [Save Frameset] from the menu bar and save the frameset as **frame.htm**. If the Save Frame dialog box (not the Save Frameset dialog box) is activated, that means you have selected a frame instead of the frameset.

7 Note that after you save the frameset, the file name is changed to frame.htm. When working with frames, it is easy to become confused as to which file is the active file. You should therefore check to see which file you are working on periodically.

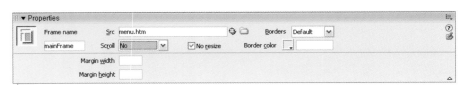

8 Select the mainFrame in the Frames panel.

9 In the Properties Inspector, set Scroll to No and select the No resize option. This means there will be no scrollbars and the upper frame cannot be resized in the browser window.

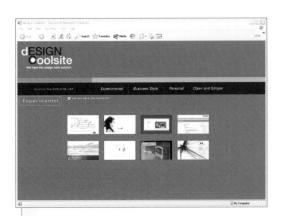

10 Press [F12] to preview your results in the Web browser. Although it looks like one document, it is actually two different documents.

11 Select the Experimental image, menu_01.gif, in the Document window. In the Properties Inspector, set Link to down_ex.htm and Target to bottomFrame. Repeat this step with each of the other menu images, linking each to their respective Web pages. Link Business Style with down_bu.htm, Personal with down_pe.htm, and Clean and Simple with down_cl_si.htm.

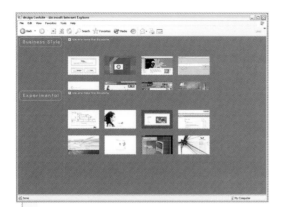

<< note

## Specifying Frame Names

When setting up a link, you can type in the frame name directly, but this could lead to spelling errors so it is always better to select from the list. Unlike many other commands, frame names are case sensitive. For example, if you type BottomFrame instead of bottomFrame, the link will not work properly

12 If you did not specify the frame in which to load the new page, the link will open up in its own frame. In this case, the link will open in the upper frame instead of the lower frame.

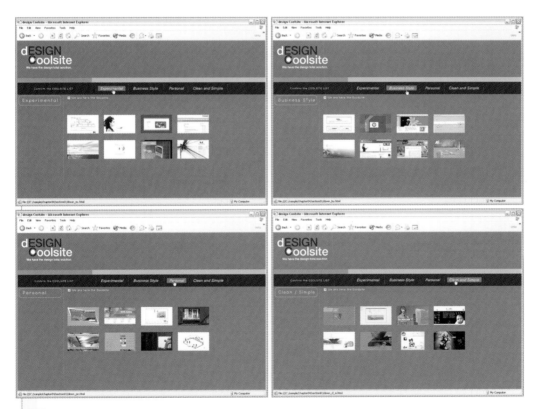

13 Press [F12] to preview your results in the Web browser. Note how clicking on the menu changes only the lower page.

# Creating a Navigation Bar

Navigation bars are menus on a Web site that allow you to go to all the associated Web pages. Designing an intuitive and easy-to-use navigation bar is extremely important, as it is the main tool that visitors to your Web site have to help them move around. In this section, you will learn how to use frames to create a navigation bar.

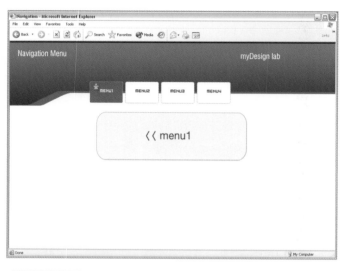

**Start File**

\Sample\Chapter04\Section02\frame.htm

**Final File**

\Sample\Chapter04\Section02\frame _finished.htm

<< note

## Resource Files

Remember to copy the resource files on the CD-ROM to your local site before you start each exercise in this book.

1 Open frame.htm. In the Frames panel, select the mainFrame of frame.htm.

2 In the Properties Inspector, set Src to navi.htm to load the file into the frame. Select the center cell of the table in the Document window. In the Properties Inspector, set Horz to Center and Vert to Bottom. In the [Common] menu of the Insert bar, click on the arrow at the side of the Images icon, then select the [Navigation Bar] icon ( Navigation Bar ).

3 When the Insert Navigation Bar dialog box appears, enter **menu1** for Element Name. Select menu_up_01.gif for Up image, menu_over_01.gif for Over image, and menu_down_01.gif for Down image. Alternate Text should be menu1 and [When clicked, Go to URL] should be menu1.htm. Set the In frame value to bottomFrame.

&lt;&lt; note

## Navigation Menus vs Rollover Images

If you click the [Behaviors] tab ( Behaviors ) in the Tag Inspector after defining the navigation menu, you will see that three events have been added. Unlike rollover images, navigation menus have the onClick event. They can also handle the MouseDown event, by which the image that appears when you click a menu item will remain until you click on another menu item. You will learn more about behaviors in Chapter 7.

4 Click the [Add] icon ( + ) to add to the menu. Repeat with 3 more menus. Click [OK] when all 4 menus have been set up. The images to be used are shown below.

| menu2 | menu3 |
|---|---|
| Menu_up_02.gif | Menu_up_03.gif |
| Menu_over_02.gif | Menu_over_03.gif |
| Menu_down_02.gif | Menu_down_03.gif |

| menu4 | |
|---|---|
| Menu_up_04.gif | |
| Menu_over_04.gif | |
| Menu_down_04.gif | |

&lt;&lt; tip

## One Navigation Menu Limit

You can only have one navigation menu on a Web page. If you try to insert a second navigation bar, an error message will appear.

**Macromedia Dreamweaver MX 2004**

Each page can only have one Navigation Bar, and one already exists on this page. Would you like to modify the existing one?

OK    Cancel

**129**

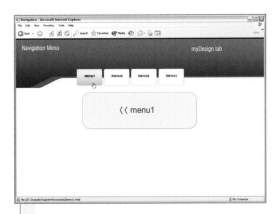

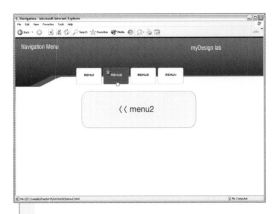

5 Press [F12] to preview the Web page in the Web browser. Note how the menu image changes as you mouse over it. This action is known as the onMouseOver event.

6 Click on another menu image and you will see a different document showing in the bottom frame. The Up menu image will also change to the Down image. Note also that the menu image does not change back until you click on another menu image. This provides a good visual cue as to which menu is currently selected.

<< note

### Editing Navigation Menus

Another way to edit navigation menus is to double-click on [Set Nav Bar Image] in the Behavior panel.

This will open the Set Nav Bar Image dialog box.

130

# Using Inline Frames

Inline frames are often used in a fashion similar to the sidebars in a printed article. These frames are often used to provide more information on the contents within the page. Unlike normal frames, these floating frames can be inserted anywhere in a document. The main downside to inline frames is that they are only supported by Internet Explorer versions 4 or later, and Netscape versions 6 or later.

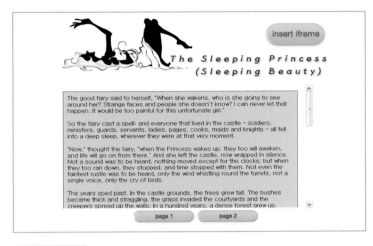

**Start File**
\Sample\Chapter04\Section03\iframe.htm

**Final File**
\Sample\Chapter04\Section03\iframe_finished.htm

<< note

### Resource Files

Remember to copy the resource files on the CD-ROM to your local site before you start each exercise in this book.

1 Open iframe.htm. Place the insertion point below the image and click the [Table] icon (▥) in the [Common] menu of the Insert bar. Set the Rows and Columns values to 1. Set Table width to 700 pixels and Border thickness to 0. Set Header to None. Click [OK].

**2** Set Align in the Properties Inspector to Center.

**3** Click inside the new table. Then right-click and select [Insert HTML].

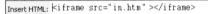

Insert HTML: <iframe src="in.htm" ></iframe>

**4** Type in the HTML code : <iframe src="in. html"</iframe>. Although you cannot see any difference in the Design View, you have embedded the in.htm document into the page.

**5** You can hit [F12] to preview the inline frame in your Web browser. The inline frame appears in its default size. You can change the size by editing the attributes of the iFrame.

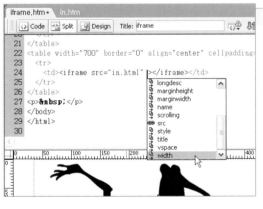

**6** Click the [Split] button on the Document Toolbar to see both the HTML code and the design. In the Code View, click inside the iFrame tag at the position as shown. Press the [spacebar], and the Hints menu will appear. This menu will help you to add the additional attributes quickly. Double-click on [width] in the Hints menu and enter a value of 650.

**7** Repeat the previous step to set the other attributes as follows: width=650, height=350, frameborder=0, and scrolling=yes.

8 By pressing [F12] to do a preview on your browser at this point, you will notice that the size of the frame is now changed and the iFrame is scrollable.

9 Place the insertion point below the table and click the [Table] icon (▦) in the [Common] menu of the Insert bar to make a table with 1 row and 1 column. Set Table width to 700 pixels and Border thickness to 0. Set Header to None. Click [OK]. In the Properties Inspector, set Align to Center. From the Files panel, drag page1.gif and page2.gif into the table to insert the images. In the Cell Properties Inspector, set Horz to Center.

10 In the Code window, type **Name="in"** inside the <iframe> tag to name the inline frame.

11 Click on the page 1 image in the Document window and set Link in the Properties Inspector to in.htm. Type **in** for Target. This means that when the page 1 image is clicked, the in.htm document will open inside the inline frame instead of a new window. Repeat the step on the page 2 image. Set Link in the Properties Inspector to in2.htm and type **in** for Target.

12 Press [F12] to preview your work in the Web browser. Click on the page 2 button and you will see the page 2 contents inside the inline frame.

**133**

# 4

# Adding Looping Background Music

Imagine being able to play some music in the background while visitors explore your Web site. With normal frameless Web pages, this background music will stop each time you move to another Web page. In this section, you will learn how to use frames to make the background music play continuously. You will also learn how to hide the frames so the Web page appears frameless.

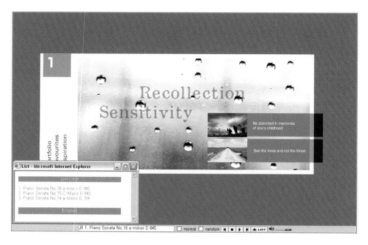

### Start File
  ● \Sample\Chapter04\Section04\top.htm

### Final File
  ● \Sample\Chapter04\Section04\frame_finished.htm

<< note

## Resource Files

Remember to copy the resource files on the CD-ROM to your local site before you start each exercise in this book.

1 Open top.htm. Click the [Frames] button ( ▥ ) in the [Layout] menu of the Insert bar and select [Bottom Frame] ( ▭ Bottom Frame ) from the pull-down list of predefined framesets. Note that there is now an upper and a lower frame in the Frames panel. Select the entire frameset.

2  In the Properties Inspector, select the lower frame from RowCol Selection. Set Borders to No and Row to 20 pixels.

3  Then select the upper frame from RowCol Selection and set Row to Relative. In this way, the lower frame will remain fixed while the upper frame adjusts to fit the size of the browser.

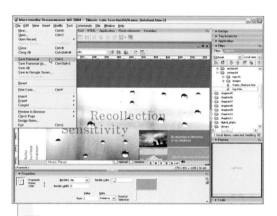

4  Select [File] - [Save Frameset] and save the frameset as **frame.htm** in the local folder.

5  Remember that the upper frame is top.htm and the frameset is frame.htm. Next, you need to set up the contents for the lower frame. First, select the mainFrame in the Frames panel.

6  In the Properties Inspector, set Src to top.htm and Scroll to No. Check the No Resize option. Also, set both Margin Width and Margin Height to 0.

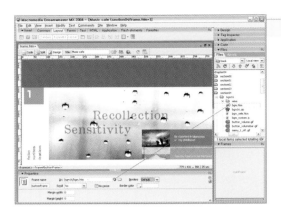

7 In the Frames panel, select the lower frame bottomFrame and set Src to bgm.htm and Scroll to No. Check the No Resize option. Also, set both Margin Width and Margin Height to 0.

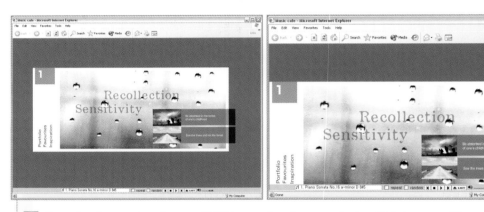

8 Save the frameset and press [F12] to preview the page in the Web browser. Then adjust the size of the browser. Note how the upper frame adjusts its size according to the browser window size. The lower frame, which provides the background music, does not change.

<< tip

## Making Frames Appear Frameless

❶ In the Files panel, right-click on the frame.htm frameset and select [Edit] - [Duplicate] to make a copy. Click the [Options Menu] button (  ) on the right corner of the Files panel group. Select Refresh. You will see the copy of frame.htm. Right-click on this file and select [Edit] - [Rename]. Name the copy **noframe.htm**. Double-click on the file to open it.

❷ Select the entire frameset. In the Properties Inspector, select the upper frame from RowCol Selection. Set Borders to No, Border Width to 0, and Row to 100 Percent.

❸ Then select the lower frame from RowCol Selection and set Row Unit to Relative. Once you set the Row Unit to Relative, the Row value of 1 will be entered automatically.

❹ Select the frameset and verify the code in Code View.

```
1  <!DOCTYPE HTML PUBLIC "-//W3C//DTD HTML 4.01 Frameset//EN" "http://www.w3.org/T
2  <html>
3  <head>
4  <title>Music cafe</title>
5  <meta http-equiv="Content-Type" content="text/html; charset=euc-kr">
6  </head>
7
8  <frameset rows="100%,*" cols="*" framespacing="0" frameborder="NO" border="0">
9    <frame src="top.html" name="topFrame" frameborder="no" scrolling="no" noresiz
10   <frame src="bgm16/bgm.html" name="mainFrame" frameborder="no" scrolling="no"
11 </frameset>
12 <noframes><body>
13 </body></noframes>
14 </html>
15
```

❺ Press [F12] to preview the page in the Web browser. Note that although you can hear the background music, you do not see the frame that is playing the music.

❻ Click on the different menu items in the upper frame. Note that the background music is not interrupted even when you move to another page of the Web site.

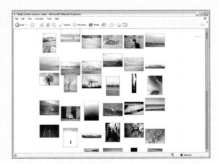

Chapter | 5

# Using Forms

Many of the sites on the Web are static; they only display predetermined information. However, the number of dynamic Web sites is on the rise. Dynamic pages allow visitors to request specific information, or submit data for processing. By these methods, a Web page becomes capable of two-way communication. Dynamic pages are usually built using forms.

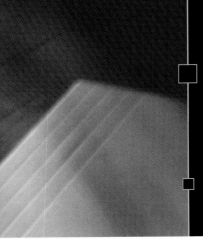

# About Forms

What do online membership forms, login windows, and forums have in common? They all allow some form of interactivity, so visitors can enter and retrieve specific information. These interactions may be in the form of text fields, pull-down menus, or simple check boxes.

## Introduction to Forms

To add interactivity to your Web page, you need to add forms and then connect the forms to a form handler, which is a program or script that processes the form information and performs specific actions based on the information. You can get many form handlers for free on the Web or through your Web hosting company.

### Setting Up a Form

1. To add a form to a Web page, you need to create a form and then insert form elements into it. First, click on the [Form] icon (▢) on the [Forms] tab of the Insert bar or select [Insert] - [Form] - [Form] from the menu bar.

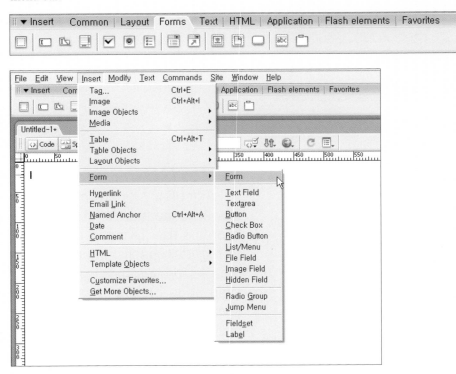

2. In the Document window, you can see a red, dashed box. This is the form to which you can add form elements, such as text fields and check boxes.

## The Form Properties Inspector

**Ⓐ Form name**: Specifies the name of the form.

**Ⓑ Action**: Specifies the address of the form handler file. You can type in the address or select the form handler file using the [Browse for File] icon (▭).

**Ⓒ Method**: Specifies the method of transmission. You can select GET or POST. Selecting Default will set the method to GET. See the sidebar below to know more about GET and POST.

**Ⓓ Enctype**: Specifies the encoding type for the data transmitted to the server. The default setting, application/x-www-form-urlencode, is usually used with the POST method. The multipart/form-data setting is used for creating forms that allow users to upload files.

### GET vs POST

GET is the most commonly used and supported method of passing form data to the server, but it has its limitations. With GET, the data is limited to 255 characters and the information, which is attached to the URL string, is not secured. When sending private information such as credit card numbers, this method is not recommended. With POST, the data is not shown during transmission and much larger amounts of data can be sent.

## Form Elements

After a form has been created, you can insert form elements into it. First, make sure your cursor is placed within the form. Then insert a form element by clicking on one of the form element icons in the Insert bar. You can also select a form element by using the [Insert] - [Form] - [Form] menu. Let's take a look at the different form elements available.

# Text Field (⬚)

You can click the [Text Field] icon (⬚) to create a text window for one or more lines of text. You can also encrypt it to protect the transmitted data.

# Text Field Properties Inspector

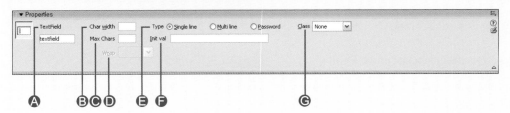

Ⓐ **TextField**: Specifies the name of the text field.

Ⓑ **Char width**: Specifies the width of the text field (optional).

Ⓒ **Max Chars**: Specifies the maximum number of characters that the user can type in the text field (optional).

Ⓓ **Wrap**: Defines how text flows to the next line. If set to Default, the text will behave according to the preferences set in the browser. If set to Off, the text does not move to the next line. If set to Virtual, the text appears to wrap to the next line on screen but the data is transmitted as a one-line string. If set to Physical, the data is wrapped both on screen and during transmission.

Ⓔ **Type**: Sets the text field to Single line, Multi line, or Password (encrypted).

Ⓕ **Init val**: Defines the value that appears in the text field initially. You should try to provide short, descriptive text telling the user the type of input expected.

Ⓖ **Class**: Used to select a style for the field.

# Hidden Field (⬚)

Hidden fields are hidden form values that cannot be seen by users. The purpose of inserting hidden form values is to make it possible to process the data submitted by the user without revealing the processes. For example, you may want the data entered by the user to be sent to multiple e-mail addresses, or to display a confirmation page after the user submits the data.

142

## Hidden Field Properties Inspector

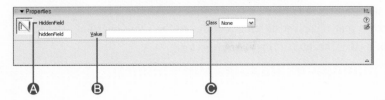

Ⓐ **HiddenField**: Specifies the name of the hidden form value.

Ⓑ **Value**: Defines a form value.

Ⓒ **Class**: Used to select a style for the field.

# Text Area (▨)

The properties of the text area form element are the same as those for the text field form element. The only difference is that a text area is set up to hold multiple lines of text by default (but this can also be changed). Inserting a text area is just like inserting a text field set to Multi line.

# Checkbox (☑)

Checkboxes allow the user to select as many items as necessary from a list, or the user may choose not to select any item at all.

## Checkbox Properties Inspector

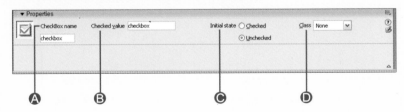

Ⓐ **CheckBox name**: Specifies the name of the checkbox.

Ⓑ **Checked value**: Specifies a value for the checkbox. This is the data that will be passed to the server or another page.

Ⓒ **Initial state**: Sets the initial state of the checkbox. This may be Checked or Unchecked.

Ⓓ **Class**: Used to select a style for the checkbox.

**143**

# Radio Button ()

Radio buttons are similar to checkboxes, but they only allow users to make one choice from a list of several options. You should group radio buttons that represent different options to the same question. The Radio Button Properties Inspector is the same as the Checkbox Properties Inspector.

# Radio Group ( )

The easier way to insert radio buttons is to use the [Radio Group] icon. When the [Radio Group] button is clicked, the Radio Group dialog box appears and you can add or delete radio buttons as necessary. Note that radio buttons added using this method always appear vertically. The Radio Group Properties Inspector is the same as the Checkbox Properties Inspector.

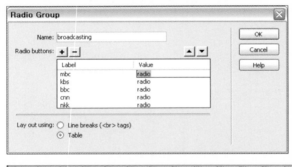

# List/Menu ( )

Besides using checkboxes and radio buttons, you can also employ lists and menus to offer answer options to the user. Using a list or a menu takes up much less space than checkboxes and radio buttons, and is especially useful if there are many options.

**144**

## List/Menu Properties Inspector

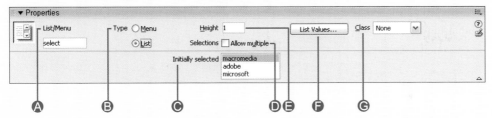

**Ⓐ List/Menu**: Specifies the name of the list or menu.

**Ⓑ Type**: Specifies whether it is a list or menu.

**Ⓒ Initially selected**: You can specify which options you want initially selected.

**Ⓓ Selections**: You can set it to Allow multiple if you want to let users select more than one choice from the list. This option is valid only for lists and not menus.

**Ⓔ Height**: Specifies the height of the list or menu

**Ⓕ List values...**: This button allows you to populate the list or menu with data. When clicked, the List Values dialog box appears and you can then type in the labels and values for all the options.

**Ⓖ Class**: Used to select a style for the list or menu.

### List and Menu

A menu is very much like the system menu. It drops down to display a list of options. The user can only select one option from the list. A list, on the other hand, is a scrolling menu that allows the user to select one or more options. To let users select more than one option, you need to select List and check the Allow Multiple option in the Properties Inspector.

## Jump Menu (⊞)

A jump menu behaves very much like a drop-down menu, providing a convenient and neat navigation tool for users. When the user selects an option on the jump menu, the page automatically jumps to the URL as requested. The Jump Menu Properties Inspector is the same as the List/Menu Properties Inspector.

# The Insert Jump Menu Dialog Box

Once you click the [Jump Menu] icon in the Insert bar, the Insert Jump Menu dialog box will appear. Let's look at the options in this dialog box.

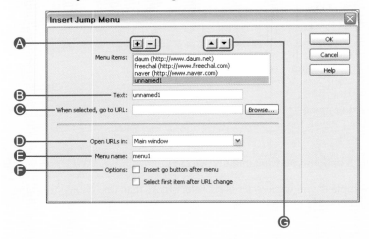

**Ⓐ Add/Remove item**: Adds or removes an item from the menu.

**Ⓑ Text**: Specifies the text label for the menu item. This is the text that will be shown in the jump menu.

**Ⓒ When selected, go to URL**: Specifies the URL to go to when selected. Both relative and absolute addresses are allowed.

**Ⓓ Open URLs in**: Specifies the link target.

**Ⓔ Menu name**: Specifies the name of the menu.

**Ⓕ Options**: You can insert a Go button so the user can click it to go to the selected URL. Checking the Selects First Item after URL Change option will have the jump menu showing the first item on the menu after a user has selected a destination from the jump menu and the destination page is opened.

**Ⓖ Move item up/down in list**: Changes the order of the selected item.

# Image Field (▣)

One of the easiest ways to jazz up your Web site is to use images to replace standard form buttons. These images function in the same way as conventional buttons, but add a touch of individuality to the Web page.

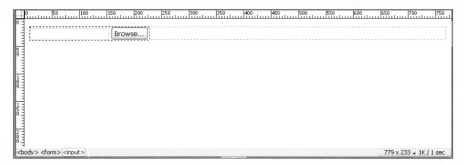

## Image Field Properties Inspector

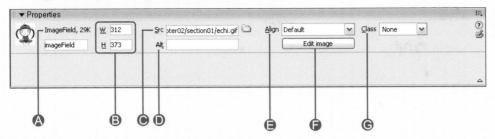

Ⓐ **ImageField**: Specifies the name of image field.

Ⓑ **W and H**: Specifies the width and height of the image.

Ⓒ **Src**: Specifies the location of the image file.

Ⓓ **Alt**: Specifies the text that appears in place of the image in case the image fails to load or the user's browser is set to text mode.

Ⓔ **Align**: Specifies the image alignment.

Ⓕ **Edit image**: Launches an external image editing program for editing the image.

Ⓖ **Class**: Used to select a style for the image field.

# File Field (▣)

File fields allow a user to select and upload a file on his computer. File fields are similar to text fields except that they have a [Browse] button so users can browse for a file. You can also type in the file's pathname.

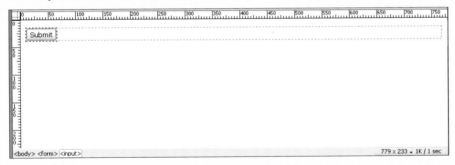

## File Field Properties Inspector

Ⓐ **FileField name**: Specifies the name of file field.

Ⓑ **Char width**: Specifies the width of the field.

Ⓒ **Max chars**: Specifies the maximum number of characters in the field.

Ⓓ **Class**: Used to select a style for the file field.

**147**

# Button ()

Buttons control the actions that take place in forms. Buttons can be used to transmit the data of a form to the server. Standard button labels used in forms include Submit, Reset, and Send. You can also define buttons for other actions as defined in the script. For example, you can also use buttons to calculate the total cost of selected items.

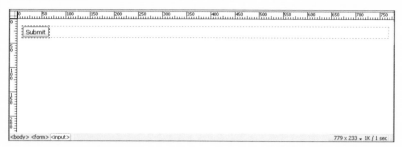

## Button Properties Inspector

Ⓐ **Button name**: Specifies the name of the button.

Ⓑ **Label**: Specifies a label for the button.

Ⓒ **Action**: You can choose a button action. The options available are Submit Form, None, and Reset Form.

Ⓓ **Class**: Used to select a style for the button.

### Setting Up the Form

If you try to insert any form elements before defining a form, an error message appears, prompting you to add the form tag first. Click [Yes] and Dreamweaver will create a form container and insert the form element you selected into it.

# Label ()

You can insert a label to make your page accessible to people with disabilities. Users with disabilities can use a screen reader (a computer program) to hear labels read aloud.

## Fieldset (□)

The Fieldset command lets you group form elements together by drawing a line around the elements and adding a name for the group in a corner. This is useful for grouping form elements that are similar. It makes the form more organized and easier on the eye.

&lt;&lt; tip

### Inset Forms Limitation

You can have several forms on one page but you cannot place a form inside another form.

## Accessing Web Pages

In Chapter 1, you learned that a Web site needs to be uploaded to a Web server in order to make it accessible on the Internet. In this section, let's have a look at how users access both static and dynamic Web pages. This will help you to understand, among other things, how users send and retrieve information using forms.

## Static Web Pages

When a user enters a Web address or URL in the Web browser, he is actually making a request for the Web page from a Web server. The term "server" can refer either to hardware or software. In the hardware realm, a server refers to a computer shared by multiple users on a network. This can be a single personal computer or a mainframe (a large computer system). On the software side, a server can also refer to software that runs on such a computer or computer system.

A Web server refers to a computer that sends Web pages to browsers and files to applications. It can also refer to software that performs such a service on the server computer. The diagram below shows you how users access static Web pages.

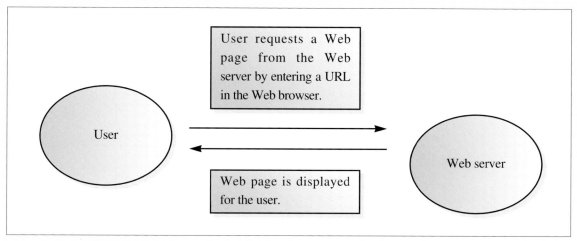

Accessing Static Web Pages

# Dynamic Web Pages

For dynamic Web pages, such as a Web page containing a form filled out by a user, the Web server processes the user's request using server-side script or a form handler before sending the Web page to the user. The page displayed to the user is said to be dynamic because it is customized according to the user's input.

For some dynamic Web pages, the Web server may send a request to a database server, which then processes the request and retrieves the relevant database information. The diagram below shows you how users access dynamic Web pages.

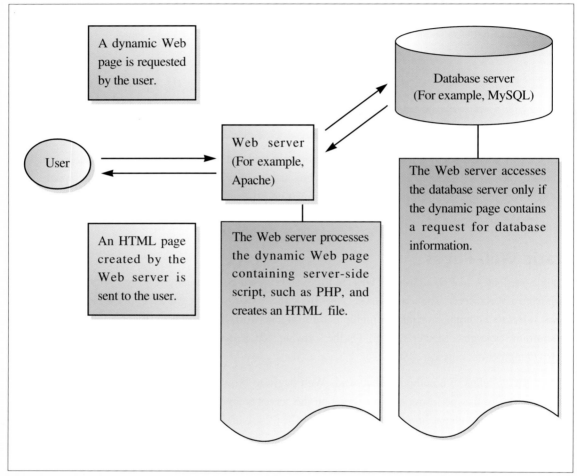

Accessing Dynamic Web Pages

## Server Technologies

Let's have a look at three server technologies - the Apache Web server, the PHP scripting language, and the MySQL database server - that are popular and are often used together.

## Apache

Apache is a popular and reliable Web server used to deliver Web pages to browsers around the world. It is an open source program and, as such, is free. An open source program is one where the source code is open to everyone for free. This makes it possible for programmers all over the world to review, share, and improve the program.

## PHP

PHP is an open source scripting language that is used to create dynamic Web pages. PHP code is embedded inside HTML pages and executed on the server. PHP can be used for retrieving data from databases, creating dynamic Web pages, placing and reading cookies, sending e-mail, and uploading files.

## MySQL

MySQL is a database server that is also free for personal use. It has many of the same features that can be found in commercial database servers (although it doesn't offer the full range of security features). MySQL is one of the most commonly used Web databases in the world. It works well with PHP on Apache servers but it is also compatible with other Web programming languages and Web servers.

In this exercise you will learn to install Apache, MySQL, and PHP on your computer.

## Installing Apache

1. Double-click \apache\apache_2.0.48-win32-x86-no_ssl.msi to start the installation.

2. Click [Next], accept the license agreement, and click [Next] again.

3. After clicking [Next] again, enter **Localhost** for the Network Domain and Server Name. Enter an e-mail address for Administrator's Email Address. Choose [for All Users, on Port 80, as a Service-Recommended.] and click [Next].

4. Choose Typical for the installation type and click [Next].

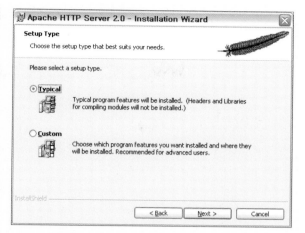

5. To choose where the program will be installed, click [Change].

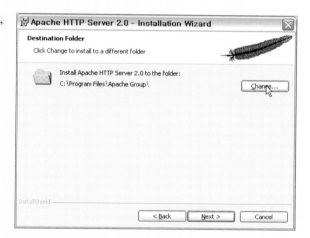

6. It is recommended that the server program be installed on the drive. Click [OK]. Then click [Next] and [Install].

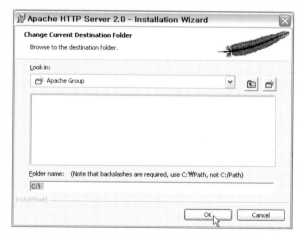

7. You will see the notification below when the installation is completed.

8. Open a Web browser and enter http://localhost or http://127.0.0.1 in the address bar. If you see the page shown here, Apache is running properly.

## Installing MySQL

1. Open the mysql folder on the CD-ROM and double-click SETUP.EXE to begin installing MySQL.

2. Follow the instructions and run a Typical installation of MySQL into C:\mysql.

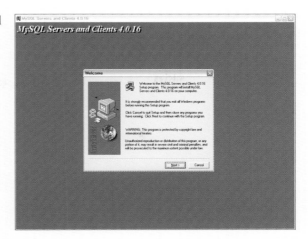

3. Once the MySQL installation is complete, the program can be accessed using the Run command. Click [Start] - [Run], type c:\mysql\bin \winmysqladmin.exe, and press [Enter]. This will start winMySQLadmin 1.4. In the future, if the e-apm0019 icon in the System Tray is green, MySQL is running properly.

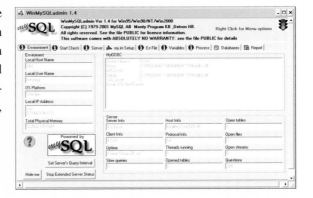

## Installing PHP

1. Open the PHP folder on the supplied CD-ROM and double-click php-4.3.4-installer.exe to begin installing PHP.

2. Follow the instructions and run a Standard installation of PHP into the C:\php folder.

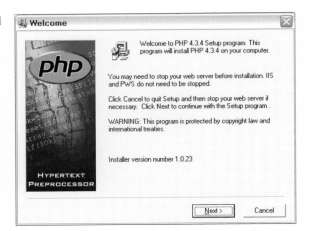

3. Enter **localhost** for the SMTP server and enter an e-mail address. Click [Next].

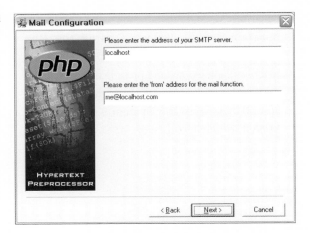

4. From the server type list, choose Apache and click [Next]. Follow the remaining instructions to complete the installation.

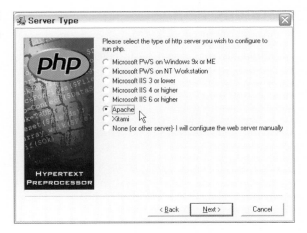

## Installing PhpMyAdmin

PhpMyAdmin is a Web-based tool that helps you to manage MySQL databases. If you don't use PhpMyAdmin, you will need to manage databases using commands entered in UNIX through the command line.

1. In the htdocs folder inside the directory where the Apache program was installed, create the myadmin folder.

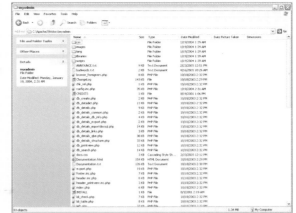

2. Open the phpmyadmin folder in the supplied CD-ROM and unzip the phpMyAdmin.zip file into the myadmin folder.

## Setting Up the Apache Server

Normally, index.html is the default file for the Apache Web server homepage. However, if you are using PHP, you must change the default file to index.php.

1. Open C:\Apache2\conf\httpd.conf in Notepad and use the Find command ([Ctrl]-[F]) to locate index.html.

2. Change DirectoryIndex index.html index.html. var to DirectoryIndex index.html index.html.var index.php and save.

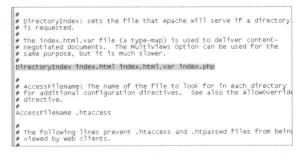

3. Restart the Apache server from the Apache Service Monitor.

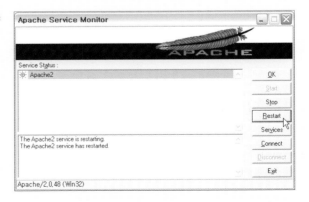

## Setting Up Myadmin

When MyAdmin is used to control MySQL, cookies need to be set up to allow access to the MySQL database. The path must also be edited so that when you login to MyAdmin, you can use the Home button to move to the first MyAdmin screen.

1. Open the \apache2\htdocs\myadmin\config. inc.php file in Dreamweaver.

config.inc.php

2. Edit lines 39, 60, and 79 as shown here.

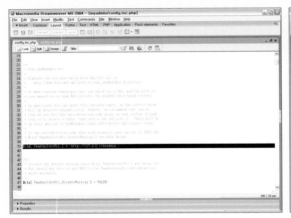 

Line 39 →
Before : $cfg['PmaAbsoluteUri'] = '';
After : $cfg['PmaAbsoluteUri'] = 'http://127.0.0.1/myadmin1';

Line 60 →
Before : $cfg['blowfish_secret'] = '';
After : $cfg['blowfish_secret'] = 'cookie';

Line 79 →
Before : $cfg['Servers'][$i]['auth_type'] = 'config'; // Authentication method (config, http or cookie based)?
After : $cfg['Servers'][$i]['auth_type'] = 'cookie'; // Authentication method (config, http or cookie based)?

## Setting Up the MySQL Password

MySQL does not come with a default password, so you need to set one up for security reasons.

1. Enter http://127.0.0.1/myadmin in the Web browser address bar. The page below should display. By default, the username for MySQL is set to root and there is no password. Log in to MySQL using the root username.

2. Click Change password.

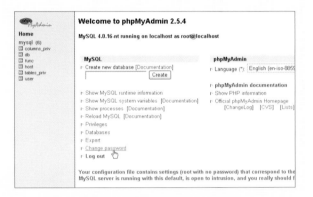

3. Enter a new password and click Change. The best passwords are a combination of letters and numbers.

4. You should see a confirmation of the password change as shown below. Click [Back] to return to the previous page.

5. Click Log out to return to the first page.

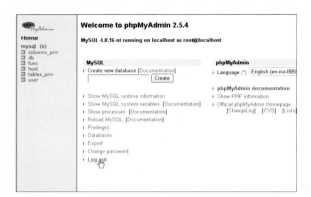

6. Enter the username root and the new password. You should be able to login.

<< note

## Program-Related Web Sites

You can visit the sites below to download free versions of the programs discussed here.

**Apache**: http://www.apache.org

**MySQL**: http://www.mysql.com

**PHP**: http://www.php.net

**Phpmyadmin**: http://www.phpmyadmin.net

# Inserting Jump Menus

Jump menus are convenient navigation menus where users can go directly to a specific Web page by selecting the appropriate option on the jump menu. In this section, you will learn how to insert a simple jump menu into a Web page.

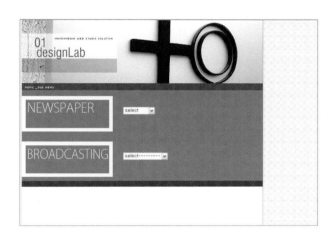

**Start File**

\Sample\Chapter05\Section01\jump.htm

**Final File**

\Sample\Chapter05\Section01\jump_finished.htm

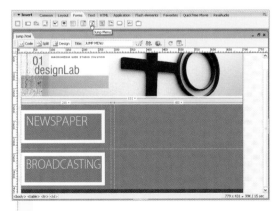

1 Open jump.htm and click on the cell next to the NEWSPAPER image. Click on the [Forms] tab ( Forms ) of the Insert bar and select the [Jump Menu] icon ( ⊡ ).

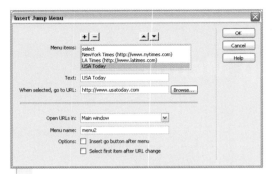

2 The Insert Jump Menu dialog box will appear. Change the text for unnamed 1 to **select**. Click on the [Add item] button ( + ) to add a menu item. In the same way as before, change the text to **www.nytimes.com**. Set up the other menu items as follows. - Text: **LA Times**, URL: **http://www. latimes.com** and Text: **USA Today**, URL: **http://www.usatoday.com**. Click [OK].

3 Note that the first item, select, serves as a prompt text for the jump menu and is not intended for use as an actual link, so it has no target URL.

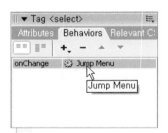

4 To edit the jump menu, you can either double-click on the Jump Menu behavior in the Behaviors panel or click the [List Values] button ( List Values... ) in the Properties Inspector.

5 If you clicked the [List Values] button, the List Values dialog box will appear. If you double-clicked the Jump Menu behavior, the Jump Menu dialog box will appear. You can edit the jump menu in both these dialog boxes.

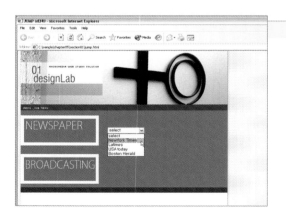

6 Press [F12] to preview the form in the Web browser. Try navigating to the various Web sites using the jump menu you have just created.

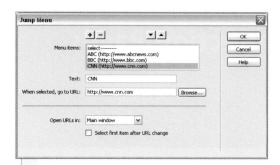

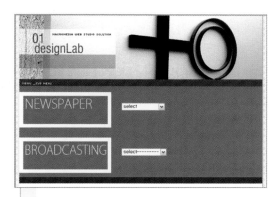

7  Click on the cell next to the BROADCASTING image. Repeat steps 1 through 3 to insert another jump menu. Set the menu items up as follows. Text: **ABC,** URL: **http://www.abcnews.com**; Text: **BBC**, URL: **http://www.bbc.com**; Text: **CNN**, URL: **http://www.cnn.com**.

8  Press [F12] to preview the form in the Web browser. Make sure all the sites are properly linked.

<< note

## Making a List Wider

If you want to make the jump menu wider, type in **select---------** under the Text option for the first item. Adding the dashes forces the menu to become wider to accommodate all the characters.

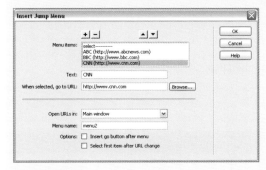

# Database Connection Pages

Dreamweaver has a number of server behaviors that can be used to connect to a database. These behaviors can be used to create dynamic pages without writing PHP code. In this section, you will create a simple, dynamic page that connects to the MySQL database. Before proceeding with this exercise, check that you have installed the Apache Web server and MySQL server successfully by following the instructions found earlier in this chapter.

**Start File**

\apache2\htdocs\user_insert.php

## Defining the Site

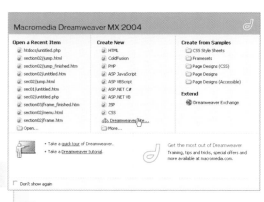

1 Define a new site by clicking on the [Dreamweaver Site] menu in the startup screen.

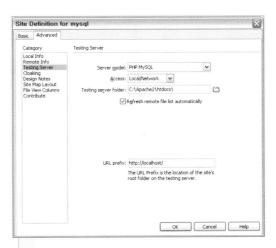

2 The [Advanced] menu can be used to set up Local Info and the Testing Server. If the default path was used to install Apache, enter **c:\apache2\htdocs\** as the local root folder.

3 Under the Testing Server category, set the Server model to PHP MySQL. Select Local/Network for the Access method of the Testing Server and select c:\apache2\htdocs\ as the Testing server folder.

4 Create a simple page as shown above. On your computer, this page should be saved as **Index.php** in the C:\apache2\htdocs\ folder. As you will only test the server connection, enter a simple line of text and add a background color.

5 The address for the Web site is http://127.0.0.1/mysql.php. If the page does not appear, you have probably made a mistake in defining the site path. Check the site path again.

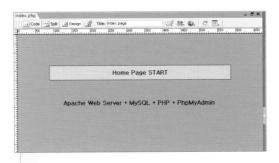

6 Enter the username **root** and the password you set up previously.

7 Type in **user_list** and create a new database.

**8** Name the database table **dw2004** and set the number of fields to 4. Then, click [Execute].

**9** Name the four fields **idx, username, password,** and **email** and set up the type, length, null, and default values for the fields as shown here.

&lt;&lt; note

## Null Value in Optional Fields

Unlike required fields, such as username and password, optional fields, such as e-mail, should permit a NULL value so that even if a user does not enter an e-mail address, his input can still be entered in the MySQL database.

&lt;&lt; note

## Required Fields

**int**: Integer
**CHAR(n)**: 'n' number of characters
**DATE**: date (yyyymmdd)
**Float**: real number
**VARCHAR(n)**: Maximum 'n' characters
**Time**: Time (hhmmss)

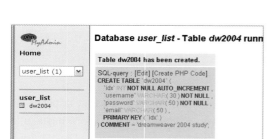

**10** After creating the table and the fields, you will receive a message that says that the dw2004 has been created. You will also see the SQL query language at the bottom. Query language tables were used in old DOS screens. In the DOS operating system, instead of selecting the items from the menu as we did here, they were typed in at the ms-prompt, which made the work a lot more time consuming and difficult.

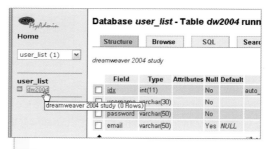

**11** You will see that the table name appears on the left. Click on the table name to see details of the table structure.

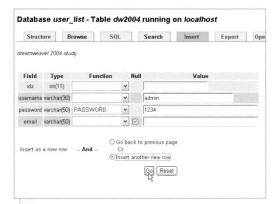

12 Select the [Insert] menu from the top to insert the data as shown here. In the Password field, set the function to password. When you do this, even the simplest passwords will be encrypted into a more complicated combination. Insert a new row (record) and click [Go].

13 This time, do not apply a function to Password; just type in a simple number for the password.

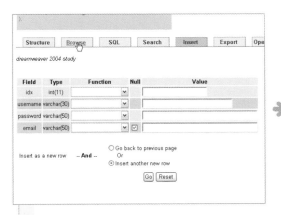

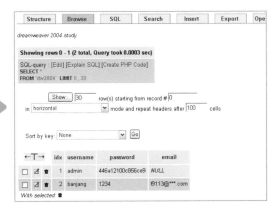

14 Click on the [View] menu to see the content you entered in steps 8 and 9. The password that you entered in step 8 (the step where you applied the password function) will appear encrypted, but the password in step 9 (the step where you did not apply the password function) will not be encrypted and, as you can see, is plainly visible. Of course this information will only be visible to administrators and moderators of the Web site.

# MySQL Connection

1 First of all, open C:/apache2/htdocs/user_insert.php. Then, go to the Application panel and click on the [MySQL Connection] menu.

2 Enter the information shown here. For the database, click on the [Select] menu and select the user_list database, as you learned earlier.

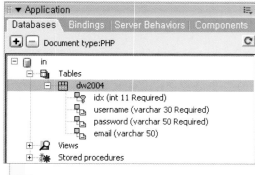

3 If you look at the Application palette, you will see the database made in MySQL, the table name, and the number and name of fields.

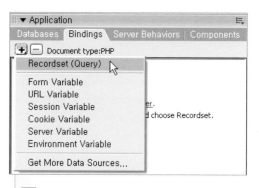

4 Go to the [Bindings] menu and click on the [Add] icon to select [Recordset (Query)].

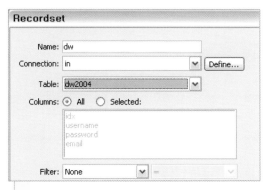

5  In the Recordset dialog box, the only entry you need to make is the Name. The rest of the information is loaded automatically from the database. Click the [Test] icon.

6  You will see the information in the dw2004 table of the user_list database in MySQL.

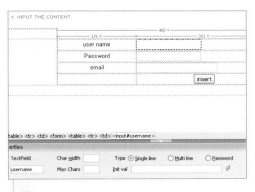

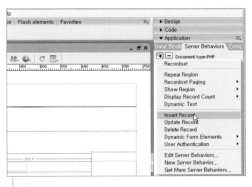

7  Select the text field in the page and see that the information here is the same as the field name for the MySQL (dw2004) table. As shown here, click on each field and enter the appropriate data in the respective properties windows. (The password type must be set to password.)

8  Go to [Server Behavior] and click on [Insert Record].

9  When the Insert Record dialog box appears, set the Connection to in and the Insert Table to dw2004. The four items under Columns must correspond to the respective field names in the Value list. Under [After inserting, go to], select the page to move to after inserting the data (Insert_ok.php).

<< tip

## Matching Field Names

If the field names in the MySQL database table do not correspond to the text field names entered on the page, the data will not be inserted.

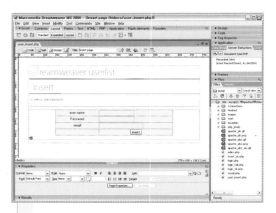

10 The area around the form tag in the middle will turn cyan, as shown here, indicating the areas that have been successfully connected.

11 Prepare a simple insert_ok.php document as shown here. This is the page that we will move to after entering data in the user_insert.php page.

12 Save your work and then preview it in the Web browser. Unlike other HTML documents, this page is one that has been created using a simple Web application. Type in the exact Web address, **http://127.0.0.1/user_insert.php** in the browser. After the data is entered, you should be taken to the insert_ok.php page.

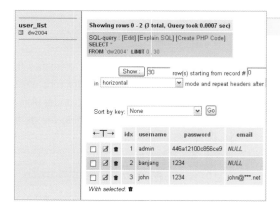

13 You will also see that data is entered in the MySQL screen. If you use Dreamweaver MX, you can create a simple dynamic Web page without knowing anything about the Web application language, PHP. Of course, if you would like to create more diverse and fancier pages, you should first familiarize yourself with PHP.

# Making a Login Page

In this section, you will create a login page for accessing the database you made in the previous section. You will need to create three Web pages–the login page itself, a successful login page, and a failed login page.

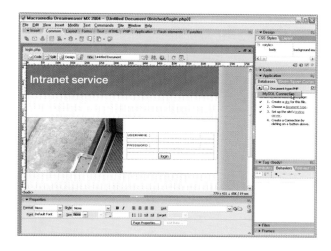

**Start File**

\apache2\htdocs\login.php

1 Open C:\apache2\htdocs\login.php and make a connection to MySQL. If you have read Exercise 2, which explains how to make the connection, you may skip steps 1 and 2.

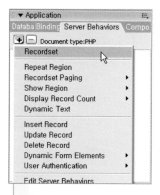

2 After setting up the MySQL connection, configure the Recordset. (See Exercise 2.)

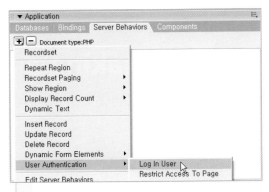

3 Type in **login** for the Recordset name. The name is for identification and has no effect on the program whatsoever.

4 Go to the [User Authentication] - [Log in User] menu.

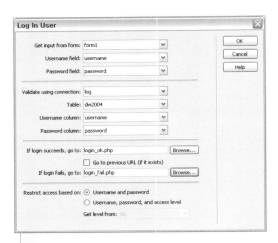

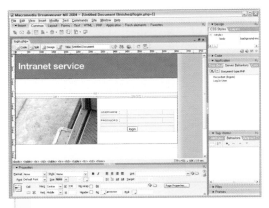

5 Set up the Log In User dialog box as shown here. If the login is successful, the user will be taken to login_ok.php and if the login was not successful, the user will be taken to the login_fail.php page.

6 After the setup is completed, areas that can connect to the MySQL database will appear in cyan.

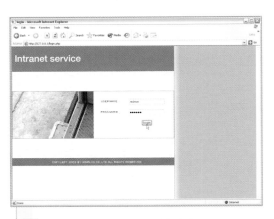

7 Preview the page in the Web browser.

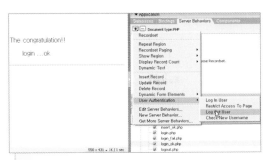

**8** Attempt both successful and unsuccessful logins to see if you are directed to the correct pages.

**9** To make the logout page, open the successful login page, logon_ok.php, move the cursor to the blank space at the bottom of the page, and choose [Server Behaviors] - [User Authentication] - [Log out User].

**10** Under the [Logout when] option, you will see the Link clicked menu. To create a menu, choose [Create new link: "Log out"]. "Page loads" is a menu that will automatically log out when the page loads. In the [When done, go to] option, select the login page, login.php, so that you will be directed there after logging out.

**11** Preview the page in the Web browser and log in again. After a successful login, you will be taken to the login_ok.php page.

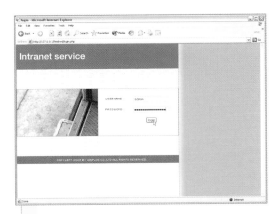

**12** When you log out, you will be directed back to the first page, login.php.

Chapter | 6

# Exploring Layers

If you have used image editing software such as Photoshop, you may already be familiar with layers. Layers in Web design are very similar in concept. You can insert layers, move them around to create the desired layout, and modify them using the Properties Inspector. In this chapter, you will learn how to insert and modify layers, and to use layers to create some of the more common layouts found on Web sites.

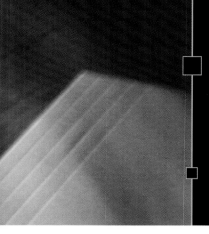

# The Basics of Layers

In the world of Web design, layers are widely used to create complex layouts that cannot be achieved using tables. Unlike tables, layers use absolute coordinates for precision placement and offer much more flexibility to create complex interfaces. Layers can also overlap and be used to make objects disappear or move across the page.

## Creating Layers

There are two ways to insert layers—using the insert bar, and using the menu bar.

### Using the Insert Bar

1. Click on the [Draw Layer] icon (⊞) in the [Layout] menu of the Insert bar.

2. Click and drag the mouse over the area on the page where you want the layer to be inserted.

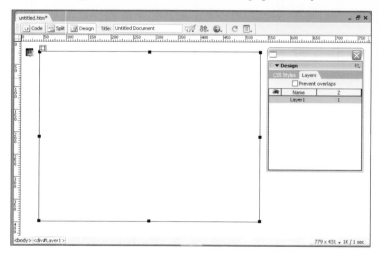

# Using the Menu Bar

1. Select [Insert] - [Layout Objects] - [Layer] from the menu bar to insert a layer on the page.

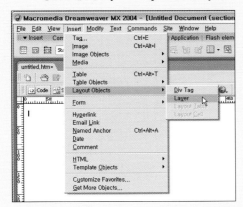

2. A layer will be inserted in the default size.

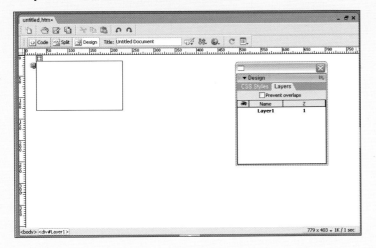

## Changing the Default Layer Size

You can change the default layer size using the menu bar by selecting [Edit] - [Preferences]. Alternatively, you can press [Ctrl]-[U] to launch the Preferences dialog box. In the Preferences dialog box, select the Layers category and change the default size in the Width and Height text fields.

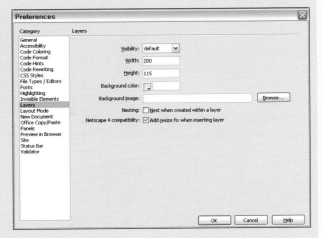

There are a number of ways to select layers.

- Select the layer from the Layers panel.

- Click on the layer marker ( 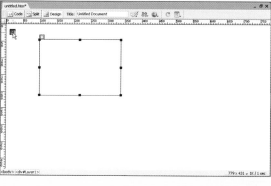 ). If the layer marker is not visible, from the menu bar go to [Edit] - [Preferences] - [Invisible Elements] and check Anchor points for layers. Click [OK].

- Select the selection handle ( ⊞ ) in the top-left corner of the layer.

- Click on the layer's border.

- Click inside the border while holding down [Ctrl]-[Shift].

### Working on Several Layers at the Same Time

If you want to apply an action to more than one layer, you first need to select the layers you want by clicking on each layer while holding down the [Shift] key. After selecting all the necessary layers, change the relevant values in the Properties Inspector. The changes will be applied to all the selected layers.

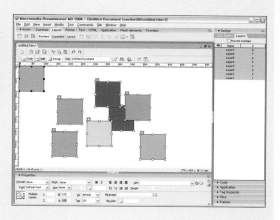

## Moving and Resizing Layers

You can click and drag on the layer's selection handle (⊡) to move the layer to a different position.

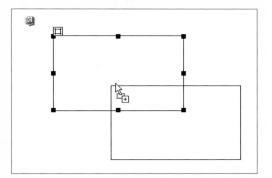

When a layer is selected, eight resizing handles will be visible. Drag these handles to increase or decrease the size of the layer.

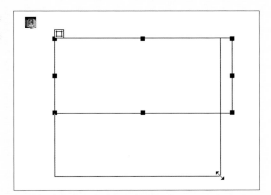

# Nesting Layers

A nested layer is a layer that is positioned relative to another layer rather than the page. Thus if the parent layer is repositioned the nested layer will move with it. Nesting is often used to group layers because it saves the designer from having to worry about misalignment, or missing a layer when changing the layout.

Nested layers may or may not overlap. Note, however, that nested layers often yield different results on different browsers. They are also unstable with most versions of Netscape.

## Nesting Existing Layers

The Layers panel displays the structure of the layers, with the nested layer indented under the parent layer. The Layers panel can also be used to nest existing layers.

1. Create two layers. Open the Layers panel by clicking [Windows] - [Layers]. In the Layers panel, click on the layer you wish to nest inside another layer.

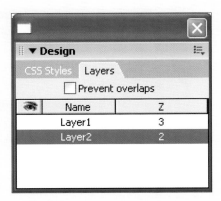

2. Hold down the [Ctrl] key and drag the layer on top of the other layer in the Layers panel. The nested layer will be shown indented under the parent layer.

3. In the Properties Inspector, note that the L (left) and T (top) values of the nested layer now become relative to those of the parent layer.

## Changing the Visibility of Nested Layers

When you change the visibility of the parent layer, the changes will also be applied to the nested layers. In other words, the nested layers will inherit the visibility attribute of the parent layer.

❶ In the Properties Inspector, change the visibility of the parent layer to Hidden.

❷ The parent layer and the nested layers will all be hidden when viewed in the browser.

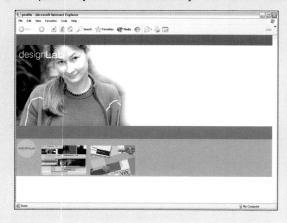

## Inserting a Nested Layer

1. Create the first layer.

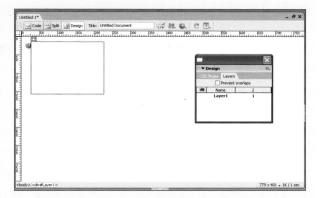

2. Place the cursor in the parent layer and then insert the new layer using the Insert menu on the menu bar–or by drawing out a layer using the Insert Layer command on the Insert bar.

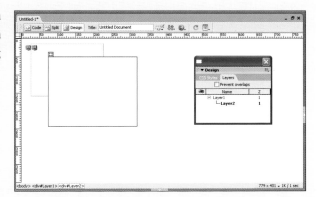

### Turning on Nesting

To create a nested layer, Nesting must be checked in the Layers Preferences (from the menu bar go to [Edit] - [Preferences] - [Layers]). If Nesting is turned off, pressing [Alt] while drawing a layer using the Insert bar will allow Nesting.

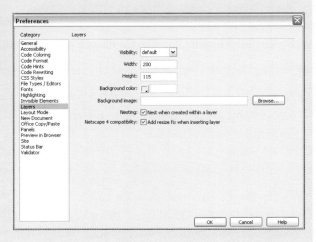

Besides changing the default layer size and turning on nesting, you can modify other default layer preferences in the Layers Preferences dialog box.

## Layers Preferences Dialog Box

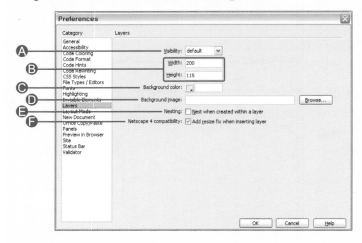

Ⓐ **Visibility**: Determines how the layer will be displayed on the screen. If set to Inherit, the layer follows the properties of the parent layer. You can also set it to Visible so the layer is shown, or Hidden to hide the layer. If Visibility is set to Default, the browser's default is used, which is usually Inherit.

Ⓑ **Width and Height**: These define the dimensions of the layer in pixels.

Ⓒ **Background color**: Specifies the background color of the layer.

Ⓓ **Background image**: Specifies the background image for the layer.

Ⓔ **Nesting**: Specifies that a layer drawn inside another layer is a nested layer.

Ⓕ **Netscape 4 compatibility**: Check this box for Dreamweaver to add JavaScript code to the document to fix a positioning coordinates problem in Netscape Navigator 4. Otherwise layers may move or disappear when that browser is resized.

<< tip

### Visibility Control Using the Layers Panel

You can change layer visibility in the Layers panel using the eye icon next to each layer. The [Eye Open] icon ( 👁 ) sets the visibility to Visible. The [Eye Closed] icon ( 👁 ) sets the visibility to Hidden. If there is no icon, this means the visibility is set to Default.

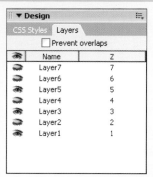

# Layer Properties Inspector

You can use the Properties Inspector to view and edit most layer properties.

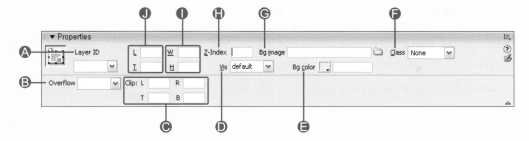

**A** **Layer ID**: Allows you to specify the layer name. When layers are added, by default they are named in sequence—Layer1, Layer2, Layer3, etc.

**B** **Overflow**: Specifies how the layer will be displayed if the content of the layer is larger than the layer itself. If Visible is set, the entire content will be shown. If Hidden is selected, the content beyond the layer borders will not be shown. If Scroll is selected, scrollbars appear. If set to Auto, the scrollbars appear automatically only if the layer content is larger than the layer itself.

**C** **Clip**: Specifies the area of the layer that is visible. The values L (left), R (right), T (top), and B (bottom) define the area in relation to the layer, not the screen. For example, in a 200 pixel by 200 pixel layer, if you want only a 50 pixel by 50 pixel square in the top-right corner to be visible, the values for L, T, R, and B will be 150, 0, 200, and 50, respectively.

**D** **Vis**: Determines how the layer will be displayed on the screen. In general, the Inherit option is used so the layer follows the properties of the parent layer. You can also set it to Visible so the layer is shown, or Hidden to hide the layer. If you set Visibility to Default, the browser's setting will be used.

**E** **Bg color**: Specifies the background color of the layer. If no value is entered, there will be no background color– the layer background will be transparent.

**F** **Class**: Specifies the style to use for the layer.

**G** **Bg image**: Specifies the background image for the layer.

**H** **Z-Index**: Specifies the order in which the layers are arranged. The most recently created layers are placed on top. You can rearrange the order by changing the Z-index. The larger the Z-index, the higher up the 'pile' the layer is placed. You can also change the Z-index in the Layer panel by dragging the layer to where you want it to go in the list.

**I** **W and H (Width and Height)**: Specifies the width and height of the layer, respectively. Note that if you insert an image or table that is larger than the layer, the layer expands visually in Dreamweaver to accommodate the larger content—but not in the browser unless Overflow is set to Visible.

**J** **L and T (Left and Top)**: These coordinates specify the top-left corner of the layer with respect to the top-left corner of the screen. The value of T (top) increases down the screen while the value of L (left) increases across the screen from left to right. Negative coordinates are also recognized. In other words, layers that extend beyond the left-top corner can be created.

Layers only display in Netscape and Internet Explorer versions 4.0 or later, while tables are viewable by most earlier versions. Web designers who want to take advantage of the flexibility offered by layers often use them to create the desired layout, then convert the layers to tables so the Web page is viewable by most browsers. However, overlapping layers cannot be converted to tables.

If you intend to create tables from layers, make sure the Prevent Overlaps option is checked in the Layers panel, then layers cannot be created, moved, or resized over other layers.

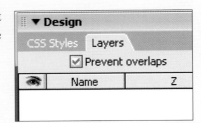

# 1

# Creating a Profile Page

A nested layer is one that has its code inside another layer–known as the parent layer. Nesting is often used to group layers so they move together, making rearranging easier. Nested layers move together with the parent layer and inherit the attributes of the parent layer. In this section, you will learn how to control the contents that appear on a Web page using nested layers.

**Start File**
\Sample\Chapter06\Section01\profile.htm

**Final File**
\Sample\Chapter06\Section01\profile_finished.htm

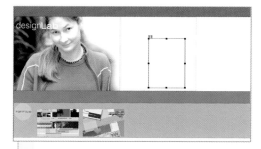

1 Open profile.htm. In the [Layout] menu of the Insert bar, click on the [Draw Layer] icon (🗐). Click-and-drag with the mouse to insert a layer as shown here.

2 Click and drag images/choi.gif from the local folder in the Files panel into the layer.

3 Create another layer by clicking on the [Draw Layer] icon ( ) in the [Layout] menu of the Insert bar. Insert images/name.gif into the layer.

<< note

## Tidying Up Your Workspace

It's good to get into the habit of making each layer the same size as the image on it. This makes your workspace appear much neater.

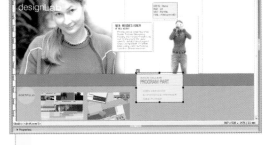

4 Create another 2 layers and insert part.gif and web.gif into each layer, respectively. Adjust the positions of the layers until they look just right. Notice how easily layers can be rearranged. If you use tables, this will be considerably more tedious, if not impossible.

<< note

## Using Grids

Grids are useful guides when you are positioning a layer. You can turn on the grids by selecting [View] - [Grid] - [Show Grid]. If you want the layer to snap to the grid, select [View] - [Grid] - [Snap to Grid]. You can modify the grid values by selecting [View] - [Grid] - [Grid Setting].

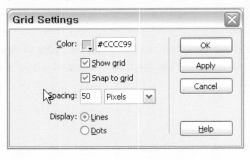

5 Press [F12] to preview your work in the Web browser.

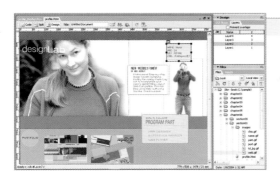

6 | In the Layers panel, select Layer2. Hold down the [Ctrl] key and drag Layer2 over to Layer1 to nest Layer2 inside Layer1. It is important that you hold down the [Ctrl] key or else you will not be able to change Layer2 into a nested layer.

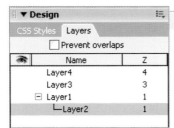

7 | Repeat step 6 for Layer3 and Layer4 so both of them become nested inside Layer1.

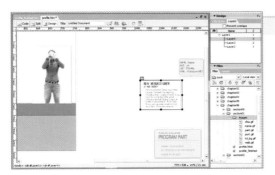

8 | Note that when you nest the layers, the nested layers move off to the right. This is because the nested layers' coordinates now become relative to the parent layer. To return the nested layers to their initial locations, select each one while holding down the [Shift] key, and then click-and-drag them back into position.

<< note

### Using Arrow Keys

When moving layers, you can use the arrow keys on the keyboard to move the layers 1 pixel at a time. If you hold down the [Shift] key, you will be able to move the layers 10 pixels at a time.

9 | In the Properties Inspector, set the properties of the parent layer as follows: Vis to visible and Overflow to Hidden. In the next step, you will notice that the parent layer is visible in the browser, but the nested layers are not. This technique comes in handy when you need to apply different settings to the parent and nested layers. Even if you select the nested layers and change their visibility to Visible, they will still not appear in the browser, as the values inherited from the parent layer will take precedence.

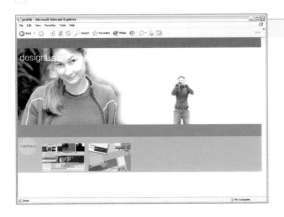

10 | Press [F12] to preview the page in the Web browser. You will see that only the parent layer, and not the nested layers, is visible. When you use parent and nested layers in this way, you can control the elements that you want to have displayed on your Web page.

# 2

# Creating a Floating Menu

Some Web pages are very long and you need to scroll down to view all the content. If the navigation menu is at the very top of the Web page, you have to scroll all the way up again to select another menu item. With layers, you can have a floating menu that remains in its position—regardless of where you scroll the Web page to. In this section, you will learn to create such a menu using layers and the Persistent Layers extension.

**Start File**

\Sample\Chapter06\Section02\move.htm

**Final File**

\Sample\Chapter06\Section02\move_finished.htm

**Extension File**

MX399281_flevpersistentDivs.mxp

MX399281_flevPersistentDivs....
MXP File
12 KB

[1] Install MX399281_flevPersistentDivs.mxp by double-clicking on the file in the Windows Explorer. This extension is needed to fix layers in place.

<< note

## Resource Files

Remember to copy the resource files on the CD-ROM to your local site before you start each exercise in this book.

Download the extension file from the Macromedia Web site. See page 9 for instructions for downloading extensions.

[2] The Extension Manager program installs the Persistent Layers extension. If Dreamweaver is already running when you install a new extension, you must make sure you restart Dreamweaver after the installation.

3 Open move.htm and click on the [Draw Layer] icon (▥) found in the [Layout] menu of the Insert bar to insert a new layer. Click and drag out a layer in the Document window and move the layer to the top-right corner of the screen.

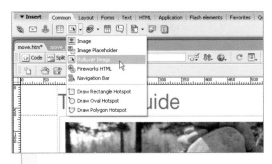

4 Move the cursor inside the layer. Click the [Images] icon of the [Common] menu in the Insert bar and, in the pull-down menu, select [Rollover Image] (▣).

5 The Insert Rollover Image dialog box appears. You will need to set up four rollover images. For the first image, set the Image name to menu01, Original image to images/menu_up_01.gif, and Rollover image to images/menu_over_01.gif. Click [OK].

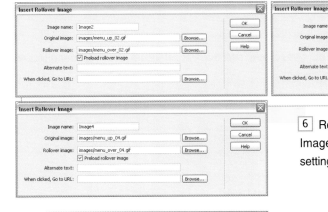

6 Repeat the procedure for the remaining 3 images, replacing the Image name as menu02, menu03, and menu04, respectively. The settings are shown in the screenshots above.

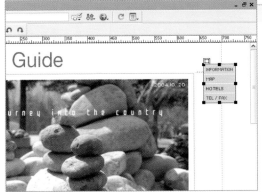

7 After inserting all the rollover images, adjust the size of the layer so that it is the same size as the menu image. The size of the layer has no effect on the page, but it is a good idea to keep the size of the layer the same as that of the images inside the layer.

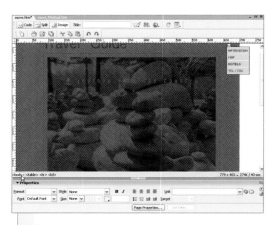

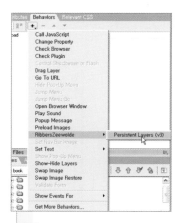

8 Select the body tag (`<body>`) from the Tag Selector. This selects the entire page.

9 In the Tag Inspector, select [Behaviors] - [RibbersZeewolde] - [Persistent Layers (v3)]. If you have not installed the extension or if you have not restarted Dreamweaver after installation, this option will not be available.

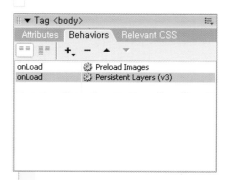

10 When the Persistent Layers (v3) dialog box appears, click [OK] to keep the default settings.

11 You should now see the Persistent Layers (v3) menu in the [Behaviors] menu.

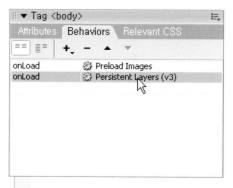

12 Press [F12] to preview your work in the Web browser. There is a scrollbar along the side, as the image on the page is very long. Note how the menu remains fixed in its position even as you scroll to the bottom of the page.

13 To select another option, double-click Persistent Layers (v3).

14 In the Persistent Layers (v3) dialog box, change Persistency Type from Static to Animated > Gradually decreasing speed. Click [OK].

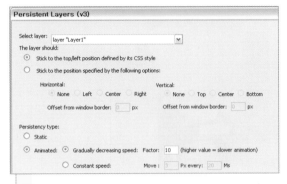

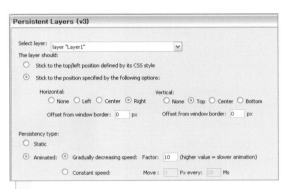

15 Preview the change in the Web browser. Note how the layer now appears to move quite naturally as you move the scrollbar. You can change the Factor value in the Persistent Layers (v3) dialog box to slow down the animation. Experiment with different Factor values and observe the results in the Web browser.

16 Next, double click on Persistent Layers in the Tag Inspector and set [The layer should: Stick to the position specified by the following options:]. This moves the layer to a specific position. Set Horizontal to Right, the Vertical to Top, and the Offset from window border to 0 px. Click [OK].

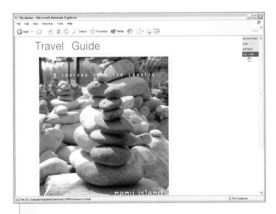

17 Press [F12] to preview the results in the Web browser. Note that the layer is now at the top-right corner of the screen. The menu layer remains there even when you scroll the page.

18 You will notice that changing the size of the Web browser will not affect the layer's position.

# Adding a Flash Banner Ad with an Invisible Background

Flash has increasingly been used to create online advertisements because of the versatility and small size of Flash movies.

If a Flash movie is added to the HTML document as a layer, the background color of the Flash movie remains visible even if it is white. In this section, you will learn how to make the background of a Flash movie invisible.

**Start File**
\Sample\Chapter06\Section03\ad.htm

**Final File**
\Sample\Chapter06\Section03\ad_finished.htm

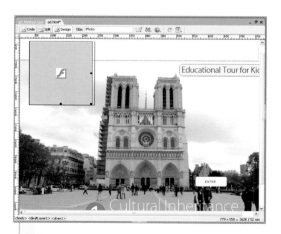

1 Open ad.htm and click on the [Draw Layer] icon (▤) found in the [Layout] menu of the Insert bar. Click and drag out a layer in the Document window. Then, click and drag images/5.swf from the Files panel to the layer.

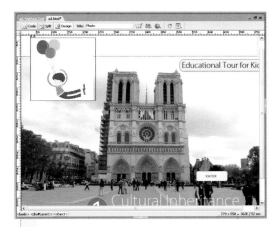

**2** Select the Flash movie and click [Play] in the Properties Inspector to preview the movie. Note that the background of the Flash movie is not transparent. It remains white so you cannot see through to the Web page.

**3** With the Flash file selected, click on the [Parameters] icon ( Parameters... ) in the Properties Inspector. Click on the + sign to add a new parameter. Set Parameter to wmode and Value to transparent. Click [OK].

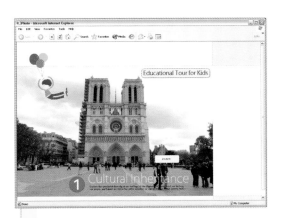

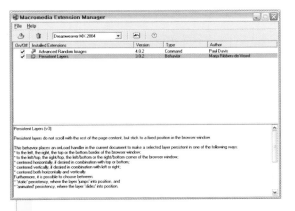

**4** Press [F12] to preview the Web page. Note that the background of the Flash movie is now transparent.

**5** Next, let's see if the Flash background remains invisible even when you move the layer. First, you need to install the Persistent Layers extension. This step is shown in steps 1 and 2 of the previous exercise.

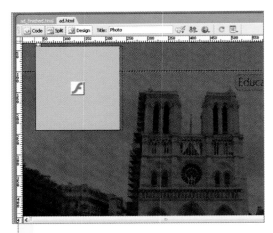

6 After the extension has been installed, you need to create a Persistent Layer. Select the <body> tag (`<body>`) from the Tag Selector.

7 In the Tag Inspector, select [Behaviors] - [RibbersZeewolde] - [Persistent Layers (v3)]. This will bring up the Persistent Layers (v3) dialog box. If you have not installed the extension or if you have not restarted Dreamweaver after installation, this option will not be available.

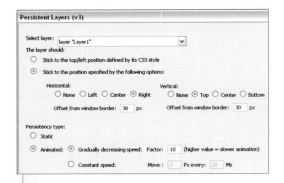

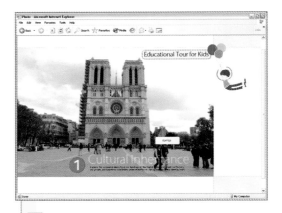

8 Set [The Layer should: Stick to the position specified by the following options:]. Then set the Horizontal value to Right and the Vertical value to Top so that the Flash file will always be at the upper-right corner of the browser window. Click [OK].

9 Press [F12] to preview the results in the Web browser. Observe how the Flash movie always appear in the upper-right corner of the browser window even if you change the window size. This kind of Flash file is used often to create banner ads for sites. (A practice which can be quite irritating!)

# Showing and Hiding Elements Using Clip Layers

The Clip Layer extension enables you to define which portion of a layer you want to display. This can be used effectively when you want to enhance or highlight only certain parts of your page. In this section, you will learn how to use clip layers to selectively display different parts of a Web page.

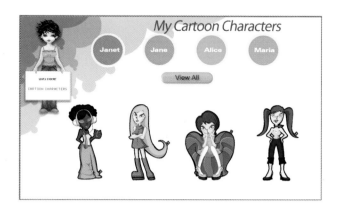

┌─ **Start File**
└──● \Sample\Chapter06\Section04\char.htm

┌─ **Final File**
└──● \Sample\Chapter06\Section04\char_finished.htm

┌─ **Extension File**
└──● MX23834_Clip_layer.mxp

[1] Install MX23834_clip_layer.mxp by double-clicking on the file in the Windows Explorer.

**<< note**

## Resource Files

Remember to copy the resource files on the CD-ROM to your local site before you start each exercise in this book.

Download the extension file from the Macromedia Web site. See page 9 for instructions for downloading extensions.

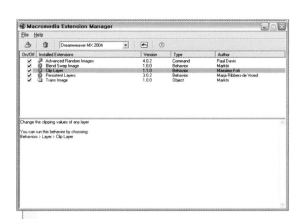

[2] The Extension Manager program installs the Clip Layers extension. If Dreamweaver is already running when you install a new extension, you must make sure you restart Dreamweaver after the installation.

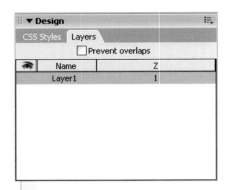

3  Open char.htm. Then open the Layers panel by selecting [Windows] - [Layers] and selecting Layer 1 in the Layers panel.

4  In the Properties Inspector, check that the W (width) and H (height) of this layer are 750 and 232 pixels, respectively.

5  There are four images in Layer 1. The total width of the images is the same as Layer 1, 750 pixels.

6  The dimensions of each image are as shown here:

| Image | Width in Pixels |
|---|---|
| images/in_01.gif | 150 |
| images/in_02.gif | 200 |
| images/in_03.gif | 200 |
| images/in_04.gif | 200 |

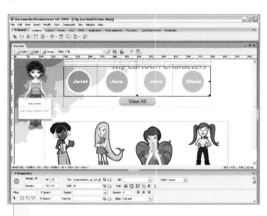

7  Four rollover image menus have already been created in images/char.htm Select the first menu images (menu_up_01.gif) by clicking on it in the Document window.

8  In the Tag Inspector, select the [Behaviors] tab. Click on the [ + ] icon, followed by [Layer] - [Clip Layer].

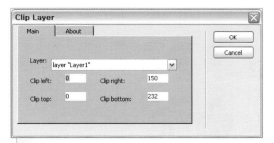

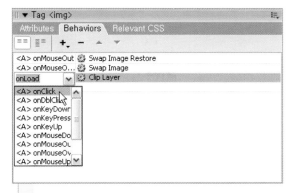

9   In the Clip Layer dialog box, check that Layer 1 is selected and set Clip left to 0, Clip right to 150, Clip top to 0, and Clip bottom to 232. By doing this, you are clipping Layer 1 to show only the In_01.gif image on the left, which has a width of 150 and a height of 232. Click [OK].

10   In the Behaviors panel, replace the onLoad selection with <A> onClick for the Clip Layer event. This means that when the image menu menu_up_01.gif is clicked, the clipped layer showing only the left cartoon character, In_01.gif, will appear.

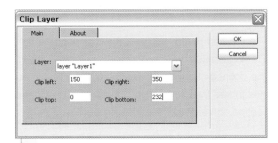

11   Select the second menu image (menu_up_02.gif) and repeat steps 9 and 10. The left, right, top, and bottom values for the second image should be 150, 350, 0, and 232, respectively. Since the first image has a width of 150 pixels and the second image has a width of 200 pixels, you have to set the Clip left value to 150 pixels to clip away the first image, and the Clip right value to 350 pixels to clip away the images on the right.

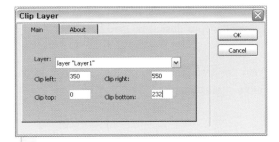

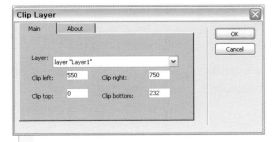

12   Select the third menu image (menu_up_03.gif) and repeat steps 9 and 10. The left, right, top, and bottom values for the third image should be 350, 550, 0, and 232, respectively.

13   Select the fourth and final menu image (menu_up_04.gif) and repeat steps 9 and 10. The left, right, top, and bottom values for the fourth image should be 550, 750, 0, and 232, respectively.

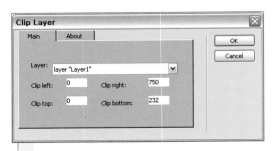

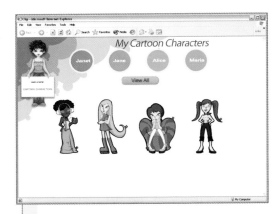

14 Finally, select the View All menu image and repeat steps 9 and 10. The left, right, top, and bottom values for the final image should be 0, 750, 0, and 232, respectively.

15 Press [F12] to preview your work in the Web browser. You should see all four cartoon characters.

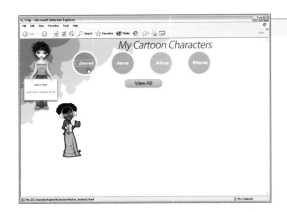

16 When you click on the first menu, you will see that only the first character appears. This is because there is now a clip layer that allows only images within the defined clip window to appear. Try clicking on the other menu images to see their respective clip layers. Click on the [View All] button to see the entire layer.

## Image Menu Organization

In this exercise, the image menus correspond to the cartoon characters in a pretty straightforward fashion. For example, the left-most image menu displays the left-most cartoon character. This straightforward design is used here to make it easy to learn the steps of using the Clip Layer extension.

When applying this exercise to your own designs, you can play around with the area displayed on the layer. You can define the area to be clipped in a more random fashion to make your page more interesting.

# 5 Adding Moveable Layers to a Homepage

Layers enable you to create all kinds of interesting layouts, but the Drag Layer behavior can even let the user change the layout in the browser window itself. In this section, you will learn how to use the Drag Layer behavior to add moveable elements to a Web page so that even visitors can alter the layout as they wish.

### Start File
\Sample\Chapter06\Section05\my.htm

### Final File
\Sample\Chapter06\Section05\my_finished.htm

1 Open my.htm and click on the [Draw Layer] icon (▤) in the [Layout] menu of the Insert bar. Click and drag out a layer in the upper left of the Document window as shown. From the Files panel, drag my_profile.gif onto the layer.

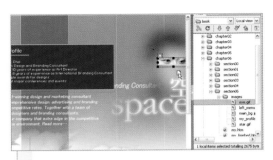

**2** Create another layer in the lower left of the Document window and drag star.gif onto it.

**3** Add another layer at the upper-right corner of the Document window and drag eye.gif into it.

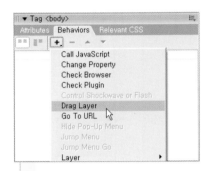

**4** It is a good idea to give layers meaningful names instead of using the default layer names. This makes it much easier to locate layers and becomes especially important when you have many layers. For this exercise, let's rename Layer1 as **profile**, Layer2 as **star**, and Layer3 as **eye**. To rename a layer, simply double-click on the layer name in the Layers panel and enter the new layer name.

**5** Select the <body> tag from the Tag Selector. In the Tag Inspector, choose Behaviors, then click on the + icon and select [Drag Layer].

**6** In the Drag Layer dialog box, select the profile layer and click [OK].

**7** Repeat step 5. In the Drag Layer dialog box, select the star layer and set Movement to Constrained. Set Up to 20, Down to 50, Left to 10, and Right to 500. Click [OK]. These values are used to determine the range of motion for the star layer.

8 Repeat step 5. In the Drag Layer dialog box, select the eye layer. Click on the [Get Current Position] button ( Get current position ) to find the current coordinates of the eye layer. This sets the Left and Top coordinates of Drop Target to 743 and 134, respectively. Leave the [Snap if Within] option at the default setting of 50 pixels. This way, when the layer is dragged within 50 pixels of its position, it will snap accurately back into place. Click [OK].

9 Press [F12] to preview your work in the Web browser. Try dragging the Profile layer around the page. Note that you can do so freely because the movement of this layer has been set to Unconstrained.

10 If you try to drag the star layer, you will find that you can only move it within the range of motion specified in step 7.

11 If you try to drag the eye layer, you will find that if you move it less than 50 pixels away from its starting position, it will snap back to its starting position. If you move it beyond the 50 pixel range, it will not snap back.

**Chapter** | 7

# Behaviors - Adding Interactivity to a Page

Behaviors are one of Dreamweaver's most showy features. Behaviors are predefined pieces of JavaScript that allow you to add interactive elements such us pop-ups and rollovers with a few clicks of your mouse. This allows you to avoid the headaches of dealing with complex code. Dreamweaver comes with a variety of behaviors, but if you can't find the effect you're looking for, more behaviors are available on the Macromedia Web site.

# Behavior Basics

The great advantage of behaviors is that they can create the kind of effects you want without having to learn JavaScript programming. All you have to do is decide which JavaScript action will work on which event.

## Structure of Behaviors

The Behaviors panel can be found in the Tag Inspector. A behavior consists of an action and an event. The action must always be created before the event. The action is a JavaScript task such as opening a browser window, playing a sound, showing a hidden layer, etc. The event is what triggers the action, for example, when the visitor clicks on an image.

## The Behaviors Panel

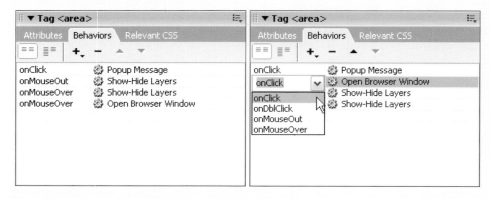

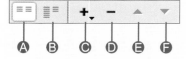

Ⓐ **Show set events**: Shows list of events that have behaviors attached.

Ⓑ **Show all events**: Shows list of all events.

Ⓒ **Add behavior**: Add a new behavior.

Ⓓ **Remove event**: Delete event.

Ⓔ **Move event value up**: change action order.

Ⓕ **Move event value down**: change action order.

## Creating a Simple Behavior

Let's create a simple behavior–a dialog box that appears with a welcome message when the page loads.

1. First, create a new document and then select the ( 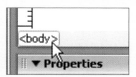 ) tag in the Tag Inspector.

2. Click on ( +. ) in the Behaviors panel and select [Popup Message].

3. In the Popup Message dialog box, type in a simple welcome message and then press [OK].

4. Looking at the Behaviors list, you can see onLoad (i.e., as the page loads) for the event and that Popup Message has been added to the action.

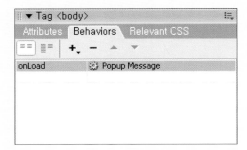

5. Preview your work (press [F12]). As the page loads, the onLoad behavior event will trigger the action and the following pop-up message will appear.

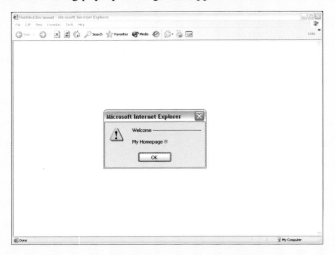

6. If you verify the source in Code View, you can see that the JavaScript has been added. Dreamweaver's Behaviors panel can be used to insert anything from simple to very complex JavaScripts easily.

```
1  <!DOCTYPE HTML PUBLIC "-//W3C//DTD HTML 4.01 Transitional//EN"
2  "http://www.w3.org/TR/html4/loose.dtd">
3  <html>
4  <head>
5  <title>Untitled Document</title>
6  <meta http-equiv="Content-Type" content="text/html; charset=euc-kr">
7  <script language="JavaScript" type="text/JavaScript">
8  <!--
9  function MM_popupMsg(msg) { //v1.0
10   alert(msg);
11 }
12 //-->
13 </script>
14 </head>
15
16 <body onLoad="MM_popupMsg('Welcome -----------------------------₩r₩rMy Homepage')">
17 </body>
18 </html>
19
```

## Applying Behaviors to Text

You can also set up behaviors so that the JavaScript will be executed when the user places the mouse on selected text. Here, you will create a behavior that will cause a pop-up message to appear when the user clicks the mouse on the specified text.

1. Create a new document and type in a line of text, such as **PopUp Message View**. Select the text.

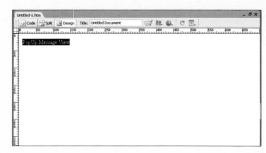

2. Go to the Link area in the Properties Inspector and enter JavaScript:; exactly as shown here (with one colon and one semicolon). This will let you apply the behavior to the text.

3. Click the [Add Behavior] button (+.) in the Behavior panel and select Popup Message. In the Popup Message dialog box, enter a simple message and press [OK].

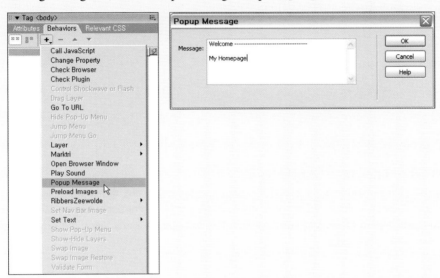

4. The event is automatically set to onClick. This means that the pop-up message will only appear when the mouse is clicked on the text.

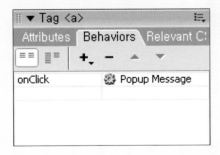

**javascript:; and # in the Link Window**

Instead of javascript:;, the # sign could also be entered in the Link box. The only problem with the # sign is that when the user clicks on the link, most browsers will move to the very top of the link page. javascript:; does not affect the page positioning and is the preferred option.

5. Preview your work in the Web browser (press [F12]). Click on the linked text to see the following pop-up message appear.

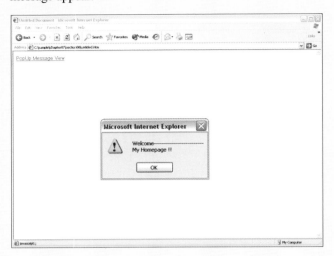

# Main Event Types

The following is a list of the more commonly used events:

**onAbort**: Occurs when the [STOP] or [ESC] keys are pressed while the image or object is being read. *Browser compatibility*: Netscape version 3 and later (NS3+), Internet Explorer 4 and later (IE4+).

**onChange**: Occurs when the entered fields in a form are changed. *Browser compatibility*: NS4+, IE3+.

**onClick**: Occurs when an object is left-clicked. *Browser compatibility*: NS4+, IE3+.

**onDblclick**: Occurs when an object is double-clicked. *Browser compatibility*: NS4+, IE4+.

**onError**: Occurs when an error occurs upon clicking a structural element or linked text/object. *Browser compatibility*: NS3+, IE4+.

**onHelp**: Occurs when the [Help] button is pressed. *Browser compatibility*: IE4+.

**onKeyDown**: Occurs when a key on the keyboard is pressed. *Browser compatibility*: NS3+, IE4+.

**onKeyPress**: Occurs when your finger is released from a key on the keyboard. *Browser compatibility*: NS4+, IE4+.

**onKeyUp**: There is no response when a key is pressed, but an action will occur once your finger is lifted from the key. *Browser compatibility*: NS4+, IE4+.

**onLoad**: Occurs when the objects of a page (images, text, etc.) appear on the browser. *Browser compatibility*: NS3+, IE3+.

**onMouseDown**: Occurs when an object is clicked once and the mouse button is not released. *Browser compatibility*: NS4+, IE4+.

**onMouseMove**: Occurs when the mouse is moved to a specific area. *Browser compatibility*: IE3+.

**onMouseOut**: Occurs when the mouse moves out of the onMouseOver area. *Browser compatibility*: NS3+, IE4+.

**onMouseOver**: Occurs when the mouse is placed on an area linked using the <a> tag. *Browser compatibility*: NS3+, IE3+.

**onMouseUp**: Occurs when you release the mouse after an onClick or onMouseDown action. *Browser compatibility*: NS4+, IE4+.

**onMove**: Occurs when a window or frame is moved. *Browser compatibility*: NS4+.

**onReadyStateChange**: Occurs when a certain element is changed. *Browser compatibility*: IE4+.

**onReset**: Occurs when a form is reset. *Browser compatibility*: NS3+, IE3+.

**onResize**: Occurs when the user changes the size of the browser window. *Browser compatibility*: NS4+, IE4+.

**onScroll**: Occurs when the user moves the scrollbar up or down. *Browser compatibility*: IE4+.

**onSelect**: Occur when the text is selected and inverted. Browser compatibility: NS3+, IE3+.

**onSubmit**: Occurs when the form is submitted. *Browser compatibility*: NS3+, IE3+.

**onUpload**: Occurs when the current page is closed or when you are moved to a new page. *Browser compatibility*: NS3+, IE3+.

# Creating Pop-Up Labels for a Product Page

In this exercise, you will use the Show-Hide Layers behavior to create layers that pop up when the mouse is placed over a hotspot. The example you will use here is a camera specifications page. When you mouse over a camera feature, a layer will pop up to provide additional information on the feature.

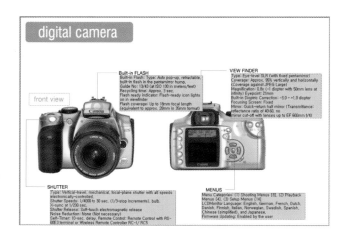

**Start File**

\Sample\Chapter07\Section01\view.htm

**Final File**

\Sample\Chapter07\Section01\view_finished.htm

<< note

## Resource Files

Remember to copy the resource files on the CD-ROM to your local site before you start each exercise in this book.

1 Open view.htm, and then take a look at the Layers panel ([F2]). You will see that this file has four layers. Each of these layers contains text that gives a more detailed description of the camera. Note that the layers have been given names to indicate their content. When creating layers you should give them descriptive names so that they are easy to locate.

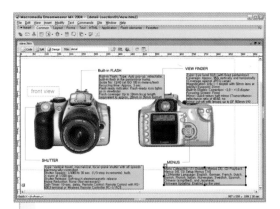

2 Reposition each layer under its respective heading as shown. Layer positioning in Dreamweaver can vary slightly from the finished page, so always check your work by previewing with [Edit] - [Preview] ([F12]).

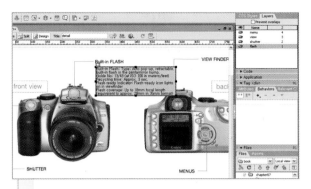

3 Click on 👁 in the Layers panel to hide all the layers. This icon is a toggle icon—clicking it once will show the layers and clicking it again will hide the layers. Although all the layers are hidden, any layer selected in the Layers panel will still appear on the page in Dreamweaver. To deselect all layers and hide them in Dreamweaver, simply click on an area of the page outside the layers.

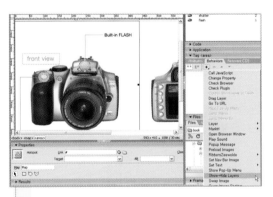

4 Click on the turquoise hotspot circle over the camera's built-in flash. In the Tag Inspector, select [Behaviors] - [Add Behavior ( +. )] - [Show-Hide Layers].

5 In the Show-Hide Layers dialog box, click on layer "flash" and change it to show by clicking the [Show] button. Then click [OK].

6 The onMouseOver event has now been associated with the Show-Hide Layers action and is displayed in the Behaviors panel.

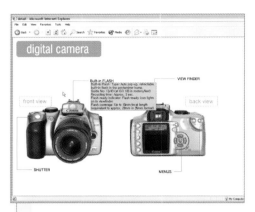

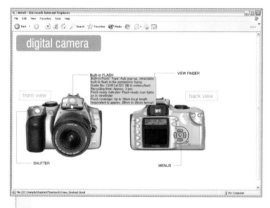

7 Preview your work ([F12]) and check to see that the description of the camera's feature (in this case, the built-in flash) appears when you place the mouse on the image of the flash. You will notice, however, that the layer will not go away even though you remove the mouse.

8 Go back to Dreamweaver and click on the hotspot circle again. Repeat steps 4 and 5, but this time set the option of the flash layer to Hide in the Show-Hide Layers dialog box. Click [OK].

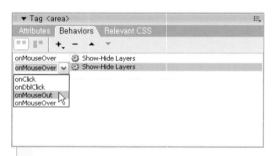

9 In the Behaviors panel, set the event of the second Show-Hide Layers to onMouseOut.

10 Preview your work again. Make sure this time that when the mouse is placed on the hotspot circle on the flash, the descriptive layer appears and then disappears when the mouse is taken off the text.

<< note

If several actions exist for the same event, the first event that was created will be listed first.

11 Repeat the steps above to add the Show-Hide Layers event for the remaining layers. Remember to select the appropriate layer (shutter, view, or menu) in the Show-Hide Layers dialog box.

# Designing a Building Tour Using Swap Image

For a simple rollover image, such as a button that highlights when the mouse is placed over it, one image is swapped with another. However, using behaviors, you can create more sophisticated rollover images in which not only the selected image, but other images are also swapped.

The finished page in this exercise will allow the user to view images of different floors of a building. The images are accessed by the table menu on the left. Placing the mouse over the buttons in the table will show the buttons as recessed and colored. At the same time, the main image will be updated to show the selected floor.

**Start File**
\Sample\Chapter07\Section02\info.htm

**Final File**
\Sample\Chapter07\Section02\info_finished.htm

## << note
### Resource Files

Remember to copy the resource files on the CD-ROM to your local site before you start each exercise in this book.

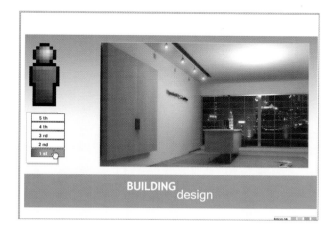

1 First, open info.htm, and then click on the [Layer] icon (▦) to create a layer on the bottom-left area of the page.

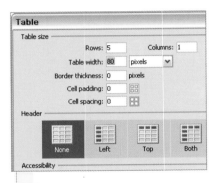

Menu_up_01.gif

Menu_up_02.gif

Menu_up_03.gif

Menu_up_04.gif

Menu_up_05.gif

2 Then, click (⊞) to add a table to the inside of the layer. Table Dimensions: 5 rows, 1 column, 80 pixels.

3 Insert the above images into the table in the order as shown.

4 The easiest way to insert an image is to drag it from the File panel to the corresponding cell.

5 Select the Menu_up_05.gif image.

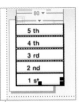

6 In the Properties Inspector, change the image name to **first** and enter **#** or **javascript**:; in the Link text field.

7 Select [Tag] - [Behaviors] - [Add Behavior] (➕) - [Swap Image].

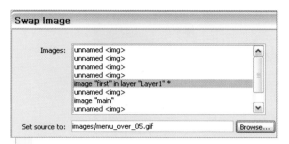

8 In the Swap Image dialog box, click on the [Browse...] button next to Set Source To and select images/menu_over_05.gif. Then click [OK].

9 Previewing your work ([F12]), you can see that the 1st cell image changes when you mouse over it.

10 Go back to Dreamweaver and select the main image as shown. Go to the Properties Inspector and type in **main** for the image name.

11 Select the images/Menu_up_05.gif image. Since you have already added the Swap Image behavior to this image, double-click on [Swap Image] in the Behaviors panel to add additional features to the same event.

12 In the Swap Image dialog box, select image "main" from the Images list. Then click on the [Browse...] button and select first.gif. This means that the main image will be swapped with the first.gif image when you mouse over the 1st button.

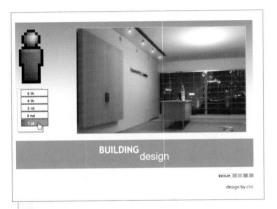

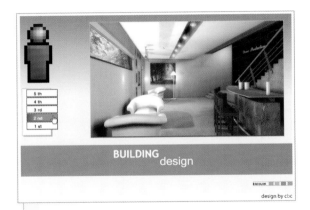

13 Previewing your work in the Web browser, you will see that when you place your mouse on the 1st button, the main visual will also change. Rollover images normally only swap one image with another, but behaviors allow let you swap other images on the page as well.

14 Repeat the steps above for the other menu buttons, replacing both the rollover button image and the main image.

<< note

## Swap Image Behavior

When adding the Swap Image behavior, you can specify more than one image swap at a time. Once a rollover image (i.e., source) has been specified for an image, the image name will be marked with an asterisk (*) in the Images list. You can then specify a swap for another image without having to exit and reenter the Swap Image dialog box. See the following steps for creating the image swaps that appear when the 2nd button is moused over:

❶ An asterisk (*) appears beside image "second" in layer "Layer1" in the Images list once the source image is set. This step sets the rollover image for the 2nd button.

❷ Next, select the main image in the Images list and set the source image. An asterisk (*) will appear beside image "main" in the Images list. This means that the main image will change to the second.gif image when the 2nd button is moused over.

# Creating a Full-Screen Web Page with a Close Button

A full-screen Web page is commonly used to grab viewers' attention, and is used mainly to create impact in online advertisements. However, a full-screen page can annoy a user if it does not have a Close button, since few users know that they can close such screens by pressing [Alt]-[F4]. In this example, you will create an opening page with an ENTER button. When the ENTER button is clicked, a full-screen Web page with a Close button will appear.

Sample image © 2003 by Min Communication, Ltd.

**Start File**
\Sample\Chapter07\Section03\full.htm

**Final File**
\Sample\Chapter07\Section03\full_finished.htm

**Extension File**
MX15317_MFX_FULLScreen.mxp

<< note
### Resource Files

Remember to copy the resource files on the CD-ROM to your local site before you start each exercise in this book.

Download the extension file from the Macromedia Web site. See page 9 for instructions for downloading extensions.

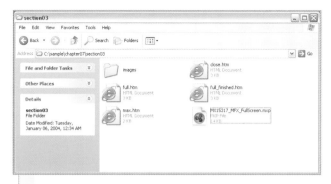

[1] Install MX15317_MFX_FullScreen.mxp by double-clicking on the file in the Windows Explorer. This extension is needed to create full-screen Web pages.

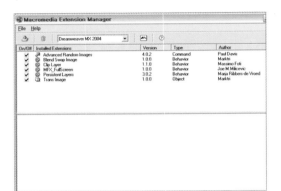

2  The Extension Manager program installs the MFX_FullScreen extension.

3  Open the start file full.htm and click on ENTER to select the enter.gif image.

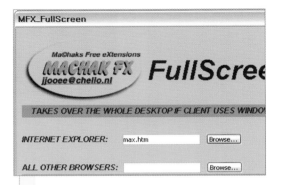

4  If you have successfully installed the extension, the MFX option will appear in the [Add Behavior] menu. In the Behaviors panel, select [Add Behavior ( + )] - [MFX] - [MFX_FullScreen].

5  In the MPX_FullScreen dialog box, click on the  Browse...  button for the INTERNET EXPLORER option and select \Sample\ Chapter07\Section04\max.htm. Then click [OK].

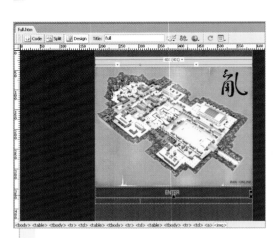

6  With the images/enter.gif image selected, enter # in the Link text field of the Properties Inspector.

<< note

## Link Option Requirement

For images and text, the Link option in the Properties Inspector must be set to # or javascript:; or the action and event options will not appear in the Behaviors panel.

**7** In the Behaviors panel, set the event for MPX_FullScreen to <A> onClick. Note that an error may result if you enter javascript:; instead of # in the Link text field. Using javascript:; is fine for opening a new window, but may result in a path error if used to activate the Close action in the max.htm document.

**8** Open max.htm and click on the Close button (images/full_close.gif) at the bottom of the page.

**9** In order to add the close action to the button, enter **javascript:window.close()** in the Link text field of the Properties Inspector. Then click [OK].

**10** Preview the full.htm document in the Web browser and press the ENTER button. The max.htm document opens up and fills the entire screen. It disappears when the Close button is pressed.

<< note

## Types of Close Buttons

The close.htm document in the resource folder for this exercise contains the following table listing a variety of JavaScripts for close buttons. Use it to create your own close buttons and test them by previewing ([F12]) them in the Web browser.

| Type | Sample | Code |
|---|---|---|
| Basic Close button | Close | `<a href="javascript:window.close()">Close</a>` |
| Click image to close | CLOSE | `<a href="javascript:window.close()"><img border="0" src="images/close.gif"> </a>` |
| Click button to close | Close | `<input type="button" value="Close" onClick="window.close()">` |
| Close all frameset documents | Close | `<a href="javascript:top.window.close()">Close</a>` |
| Click image to close frameset document | CLOSE | `<a href="javascript:top.window.close()"><img border="0" src="images/close.gif"></a>` |
| Click button to close frameset document | Close | `<input type="button" value="Close" onClick="top.window.close()">` |

# 4

# Creating Pop-Up Ads that Open in a New Window

Pop-up ads that open in a new, smaller window are commonly found on the Web these days. Some ads will open in a new window as soon as the main Web page is loaded while others will open only if the user clicks on a link. In this exercise, you will learn to create a pop-up window using the Open Browser Window behavior.

**Start File**
\Sample\chapter07\section04\open.htm

**Final File**
\Sample\chapter07\section04\open_finished.htm

<< note

## Resource Files

Remember to copy the resource files on the CD-ROM to your local site before you start each exercise in this book.

1 Open the start file open.htm and select the <body> tag from the Tag Selector. This will select the entire page.

3 In the Open Browser Window dialog box, click on the [Browse...] button of the [URL to Display] option and select the new.htm file. Set both Window width and Window height to 300 pixels. Do not select any of the six attributes. Enter **new** for the Window name. Window names cannot contain spaces or special characters.

2 Click the [Add Behavior] button (+.) in the Behaviors panel and select [Open Browser Window].

4 In the Behaviors panel, you will notice that the onLoad event is associated with the Open Browser Window action. This means that the event will occur immediately upon opening a page.

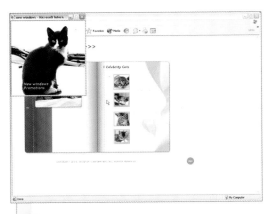

5 Preview your work in the Web browser ([F12]). When the page opens, the onLoad event causes a new 300 × 300 page to open.

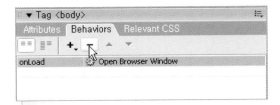

6 Now you will change the page so that the new window only appears when the NEW button is selected. Click on the <body> tag in the Tag Selector. With the Open Browser Window action selected in the Behaviors panel, click on the [Remove event] button.

[7] Click on the NEW button image at the bottom of the page. In the Behaviors panel, click on the [Add Behavior] button (⊞) and select [Open Browser Window].

[8] In the Open Browser Window dialog box, select the [Scrollbars as needed] and [Resize handles] attributes. All other values should be the same as before. The Resize handles attribute lets the user adjust the size of the new window, while the Scrollbars as needed attribute adds a scrollbar.

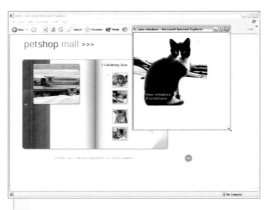

[9] Set the event to <A> onClick.

[10] Preview your work in the Web browser ([F12]). This time the new window appears only when the NEW image at the bottom of the page is clicked.

&lt;&lt; note

## When the ⟨A⟩ onClick Option Is Not Available

This is most likely because the # link has been omitted. Simply select the image, enter # in the Link field in the Properties Inspector, and press [Enter].

# 5 Using the Change Properties Behavior

In this exercise, you will learn to use the Change Properties behavior to create the effect of changing another image when an image is clicked. You will add rollover images to the menu of a boys apparel page of a clothing store. When a menu item is clicked, the image of the cartoon model changes. You will also add show and hide buttons that will let you show or hide the model.

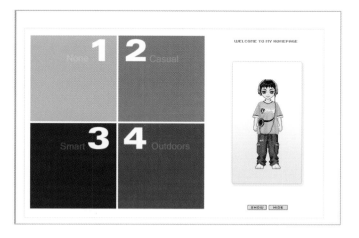

**Start File**

\Sample\Chapter07\Section05\property.htm

**Final File**

\Sample\Chapter07\Section05\property_finished.htm

<< note

## Resource Files

Remember to copy the resource files on the CD-ROM to your local site before you start each exercise in this book.

[1] Open the start file, property.htm. The file contains four rollover menu images (1, 2, 3, 4) and one cartoon model. Mouse over the menu images and you will see the words None, Casual, Smart, or Outdoors light up. Because rollover events have already been applied to the four menu images, they have a # entry in the Link field and an image name in the Properties Inspector.

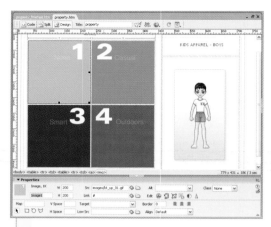

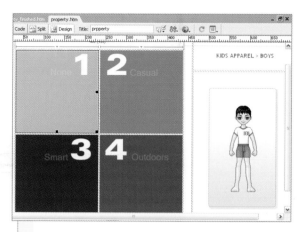

2 Let's name the cartoon. Click on the cartoon and type in **model** for the image name in the Properties Inspector.

3 Click on the 1 menu image (images/bt_up_01.gif) and then, in the Behaviors panel, click on the [Add Behavior] button (+) and select [Change Properties].

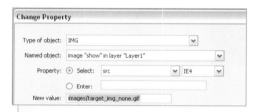

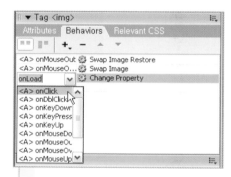

4 In the Change Properties dialog box, select IMG under [Type of object] to indicate that this is an image. Select image "model" under [Named object] to choose the cartoon, and enter **images/target_img_none.gif** in the New value field.

5 If the event is set to onLoad in the Behaviors panel, change it to <A> onClick.

6 Repeat steps 3 to 5 for the other menu images. In the [New value] field of the Change Properties dialog box, enter **images/target_img_ casual.gif** for the 2 menu image, **images/ target_ img_smart.gif** for the 3 menu image, and **images/target_img_outdoors.gif** for the 4 menu image.

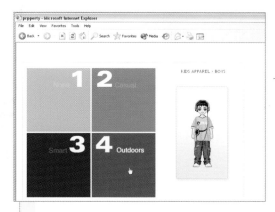

7 Preview your work so far in the Web browser ([F12]). You will see that when a menu image is clicked, the cartoon model will change.

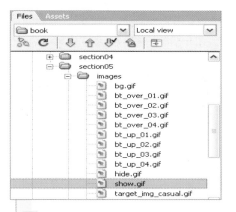

8 Now let's create Show and Hide buttons that will show or hide the cartoon. First, click to the right of the cartoon and press [Enter] five or six times to move the cursor down the page. Then insert the show.gif and hide.gif images below the cartoon by dragging show.gif, and then hide.gif, from the Files panel.

<< note

## Setting Up the Rollover

To make the cartoon a rollover image, you will need to change the events of all four menu images to <A> onMouseOver. Then the cartoon image will change when the mouse is placed over the menu images.

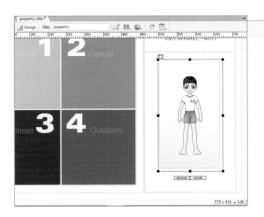

9 In the [Layout] Insert bar, select the [Draw Layer] button ( ) and draw a small layer somewhere on the screen. Drag the cartoon into the layer–the layer will expand to fit the image–and position the layer back to where the image was. Remember to place only the cartoon inside in the layer, and not the Show or Hide button images.

10 With the layer selected, you will see in the Properties Inspector that the name of the layer is set to Layer1.

11 Now select the Show button image and enter # in the Link field in the Properties Inspector.

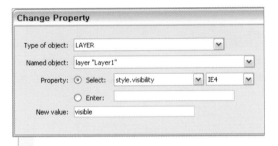

12 With show button selected go to the Behaviors panel, click on the [Add Behavior] button ( +. ), and select [Change Properties].

13 Select LAYER for [Type of object] and "Layer1" for [Named object]. If the "Layer1" option does not appear, try selecting another Type of Object–for example, IMG–and then select LAYER again. Under Properties, check the Select radio button, select style.visibility, and make sure it is set for versions later than IE4. Finally, enter **visible** for [New value], and click [OK].

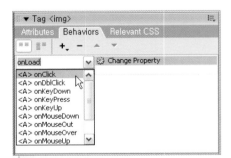

14 In the Behaviors panel, change the event from <A> onLoad to <A> onClick.

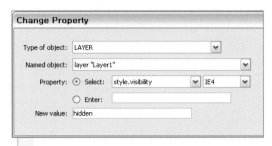

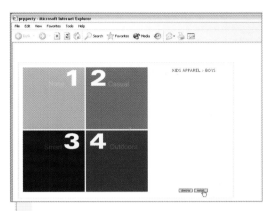

15 Now select the Hide button image and repeat steps 12, 13, and 14. However, in step 13, set the [New value] in the Change Properties dialog box to **hidden**.

16 Preview your work in the Web browser. Click on the Show or Hide buttons to display or hide the layer that contains the cartoon.

Chapter | 8

# The Assets Panel - Using Libraries and Templates

When working with large sites, it can be hard to keep track of the many elements that were used in creating the Web pages. The Assets panel can help you organize these elements and make it easy to insert the same elements over and over again. Among the assets in the panel are the library items and templates; these allow you to reuse and update elements and page designs across the entire site with a single command.

# The Assets Panel

The Assets panel is rather like a file manager, but unlike the Files panel, it displays the files or elements used in your site by type and not in a hierarchical directory. The Assets panel lets you categorize and group your assets, such as images and media files, making them easy to find and manage.

## Using the Assets Panel

The Assets panel can be found in the Files panel group, or you can access it by hitting the [F11] shortcut key. There are nine different categories of assets, each accessible by clicking on the relevant button on the left of the Assets panel. Let's look at these asset categories and learn to add the assets on your Web site to a list of favorite assets.

### The Assets Panel

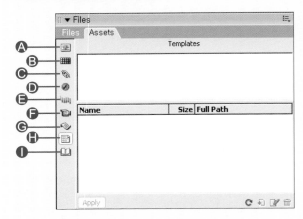

Ⓐ **Image** (▣): Displays image files—such as those in the GIF, JPEG, or PNG format—that are found in your site folder. Images can be arranged by name, file size, file type, or directory path.

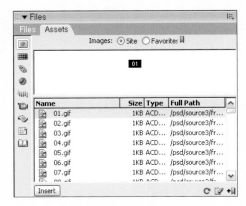

**B** **Colors** (▦): Shows all the colors (text color, background color, etc.) used in your Web site.

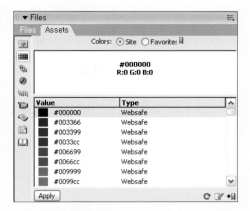

**C** **URLs** (✎): Shows all the external links in your Web site. URLs include HTTP, HTTPS, FTP, JavaScript, email (mailto:), and local file (file://) links.

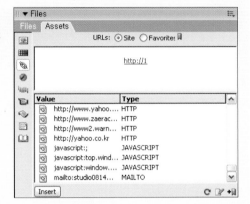

**D** **Flash** (◉): Shows Macromedia Flash movies (SWF) but not the FLA source files.

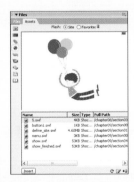

**E** **Shockwave** (▥): Shows Shockwave movies created with Director or Authorware.

**F** **Movies** (▤): Lists Apple QuickTime or MPEG movies.

**G** **Scripts** (✎): Shows JavaScript or VBScript files. Scripts that are contained in HTML files, as opposed to independent JavaScript or VBScript files, do not appear in the Assets panel.

**H** **Templates** (▤): Templates are used to apply the same page layout to several pages. You can modify the layout for all pages simply by modifying the template.

**I** **Library** (▥): You can place page elements that you intend to use on several pages into the Library category. Assets in the Library category are known as library items. Changing a library item will update the item in all pages that use the element.

## Applying Assets

1. Select an asset category from the left of the Assets panel.

2. On the Web page, check that your cursor is placed at the point where you want to insert the asset or select the elements that you want to apply the asset to (such as a color).

3. In the Assets panel, select the name of the asset and click on the Insert or Apply button.

4. The asset will be inserted or applied to the Web page.

## Adding Assets to a List of Favorites

The larger your Web site, the greater the number of assets you'll have to deal with. To make it easy to find and insert commonly used assets, you can add these assets to a list of favorites. Using the favorites list can help you save a lot of time.

1. In the Assets panel, right-click on an element you often use and choose [Add to Favorites] from the shortcut menu, or click on the command's icon (⬚).

2. Click on the Favorite radio button at the top of the panel. You will see the element added in the relevant category of the list of favorite assets.

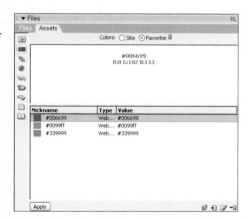

# Using the Library

As you build a Web site, you will tend to reuse similar forms, images, or text to achieve a uniform look in your Web pages. The library makes using these repeated elements easier.

1. Click on the [Library] icon (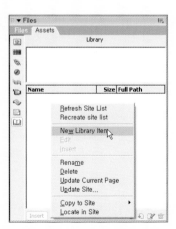). You will see that there are no items in the library. Right-click on the empty assets list and select [New Library Item].

2. A new item will be added. Name it **600-px-table** and then hit [Enter]. Next, either double-click this item or right-click on it and select [Edit]. The 600-px-table.lbi library file will open in the Document window.

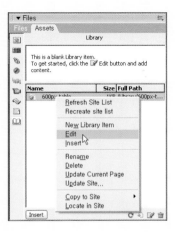

3. Now let's insert a table into the library file. Using the Insert bar, or by selecting [Insert] - [Table] from the main menu, insert a 1-row, 1-column table with a table width of 600 pixels, as shown here. Click [OK]. In the main menu, click [File] - [Save].

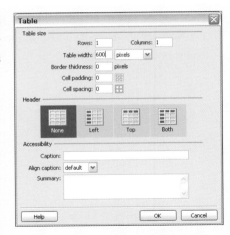

4. Now click on the [Files] tab of the Files panel, and you can see that in the local folder for the site a Library folder has been created. The table you just created is in the 600px-table.lbi file in the Library folder.

5. To use the library item you created, open a new document, and—from the Assets panel—drag the 600px-table asset onto the page to insert the library item. The new table cannot be modified on the Web page, but you can make changes to it in the library file.

6. Now open the library item 600px-table.lbi. Right-click on the table and choose [Table] - [Select Table]. In the Properties Inspector, change the Width to 700 pixels and Background color to #CC6633.

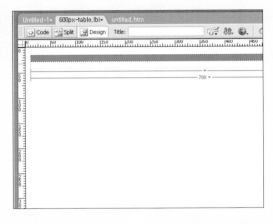

234

7. You must now save the item or the changes will not be applied to the Web page. Click [File] - [Save]. All the documents that use the table will be updated.

<< note

### Excluding Items from the Library

If you added a library item to a page but want it to stand alone, select the item on the Web page and then click on [Detach from original] in the Properties Inspector. It can now be edited independently of the library item.

## Using Templates

Commonly used Web page layouts can be made into templates. With templates you can quickly create or update any number of pages with the same layout. Let's suppose that you need to create 100 pages with the same layout, and then modify the layout for all the pages. Without templates, each of the 100 pages would have to be edited individually. By using templates, however, modifications to the master template can be automatically applied to all 100 pages. In this section, you will learn how to create templates.

1. In order to make a template, you need to open a new document or open an existing one. For this exercise, let's use the example file \Sample\Chapter08\Section00 \tem.htm which contains some text and a table.

2. As with library items, you can create a template in the Assets panel by selecting the Template category, right-clicking on the assets list, and then selecting [New Template] from the shortcut menu. However, the Insert bar is easier to use. From the Insert bar, select the [Common] menu, then the [Templates] icon ( ). Click [Make Template].

3. In the Save As Template dialog box, the file name "tem" appears in the Save as field. Click [Save] to name the template **tem** as well.

4. Check in the Files panel to see that the Templates folder has been created and it contains the tem.dwt template file.

&lt;&lt; note

## Moving Template and Library Folders

If the Templates folder is moved inside another folder, the templates will no longer work properly. The same goes for Library folders. Although they will still appear in the Assets panel you won't be able to use their items if they are moved to other folders.

5. When the template is created, you will notice that the template file has the extension .dwt. DWT files, like HTML documents, are editable.

6. Now select [File] - [New] from the main menu to create a new document.

7. In the New from Template dialog box, select the [Templates] tab, which displays the names of all the sites saved on the computer and the templates for each site. Click on the template you just made, tem, and then choose [Create] to apply this template to the new document.

8. You now have a new, unsaved document based on the template. The words [template:tem] in the top-right corner of the document indicate that the template has been applied.

## Applying Templates to Existing Files

1. Using the Files panel, open an existing file. Now click on the [Assets] tab in the Files panel, choose the template, and drag it onto the page to apply it.

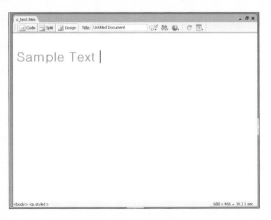

2. If the page already contains other elements, such as text or tables, the Inconsistent Region Names dialog box will appear. Click on the name of an editable region such as the Document Body, and select [Nowhere] in the Move Content to New Region option. Click on the [Use for All] button to apply the setting to all editable regions. Click [OK].

3. This will remove all existing elements from the page.

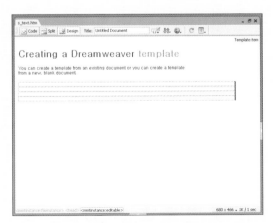

## Updating Templates

Templates can be edited when modifications are needed.

1. Edit the tem.dwt file by making simple modifications to the cell color, table size, and number of rows.

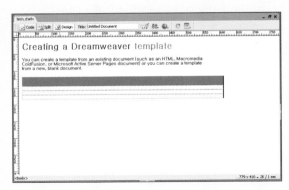

2. After making the changes, press [Ctrl]-[S] to save your changes. A warning will appear, telling you that the template does not have any editable regions. For now, click [OK] to save.

3. Once you save the changes, all Web pages to which the tem.dwt file has been applied will be updated with the new information. If this does not happen automatically, choose [Modify] - [Templates] - [Update Pages] from the main menu.

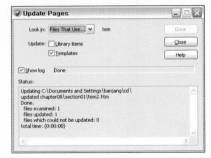

4. After updating, you can check the result in a page created with the template. You will find that no matter where you click on the page, you won't find any editable regions. In the next section, you will learn to add editable regions

## Adding Editable Regions to Templates

When documents are first created from a template, they will be made without any regions that can be edited by the user. To edit the template, you must add editable regions.

1. In the tem.dwt template file, place the cursor into the table as shown. With the [Common] menu selected in the Insert bar, click and hold on the [Templates] icon () and select [Editable Region].

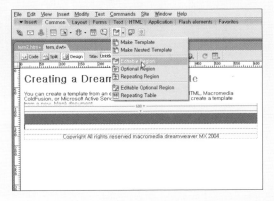

2. In the New Editable Region dialog box, enter the name **insert**. Click [OK]. A new editable region will be created.

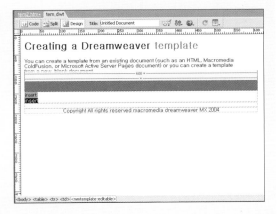

3. The name insert appears to indicate that it is an editable region. You must save the template in order to apply this change to all pages that are based on the template.

4. Open a Web page that uses this template and type in text at the Insert marker, then press [Enter]. The cell will expand to accommodate the text. Only the editable cell can be modified while the rest of the page stays the same.

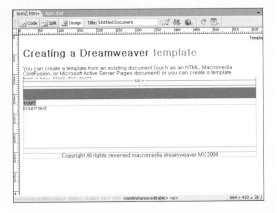

**239**

# Using Templates to Create and Update Several Pages

In this exercise, you will practice using templates to create a consistent layout on a few Web pages. You will experience first-hand how creating and updating layouts and links can be done quickly and easily using templates. In addition, you will also learn to add and remove editable regions from templates.

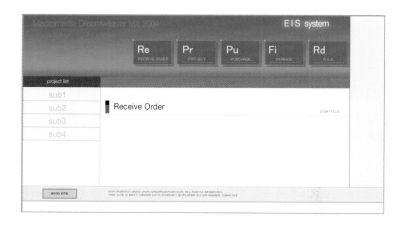

**Start File**

\Sample\Chapter08\Section01\product.htm

<< note

## Resource Files

Remember to copy the resource files on the CD-ROM to your local site before you start each exercise in this book.

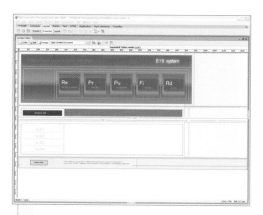

1 Open the start file, product.htm. First, let's examine the layout of this file. In the Insert bar, select the [Layout] category and click on the [Expanded] button to view the file in the Expanded Tables mode. You will see this document has a very complex nested table structure. If you've followed the examples in this book thus far, you should have no trouble making these kinds of tables.

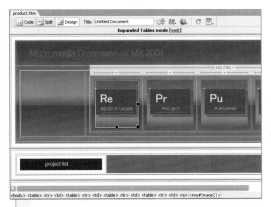

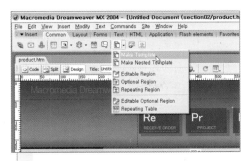

2 To analyze the table structure, click on an image or a cell and then go to the Tag Selector at the bottom of the Document window. Click on the tags from right to left to view the selected element in the Document window and see its properties in the Properties Inspector. Then work your way out through the other tables. You should make templates for complex layouts such as this one because using templates will save you a lot of time.

3 In the [Common] category of the Insert bar, click on the [Templates] icon ( ) and select [Make Template].

4 In the Save As Template dialog box, name the template **eis**. Select the name of your current local site in the [Site] drop-down menu. Click [Save] to create the eis.dwt template

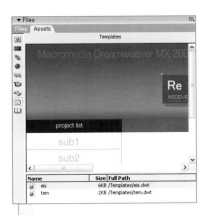

5 You can preview the template in the Assets panel by selecting [eis].

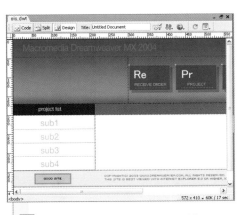

6 Later on, you will set the white space beside the submenu buttons as an editable area where you can insert contents. First, let's do something about the layout of the white space. Click in the white space and click on the [Table] button ( ) on the Insert bar to insert a table.

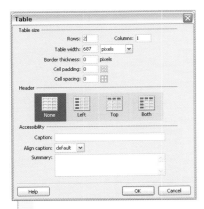

7 In the Table dialog box, set the Table width to 687 pixels with 2 rows and 1 column. Border thickness, Cell padding, and Cell spacing must all be set to 0. Click [OK].

8 You will use this table to insert a header image. In the Files panel, drag the title1.gif image to the bottom cell of this table. The image is not inserted into the top cell because the top cell can be used to fine-tune the image's vertical placement.

9 Now let's add a table beneath the Receive Order image. Select the table containing the image and then insert a table by clicking on the [Table] button (⊞) in the Insert bar. Selecting a complex table before inserting a new table will create the new table below the complex table.

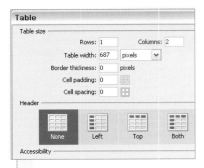

10 In the Table dialog box, insert the settings 1 row, 2 columns, and a width of 687 pixels.

11 As shown here in the Properties Inspector, set the size of the left cell to 50 pixels and the right cell to 637 pixels. The widths of these two cells add up to the total table width of 687 pixels.

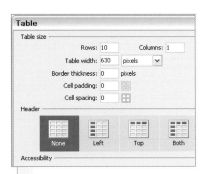

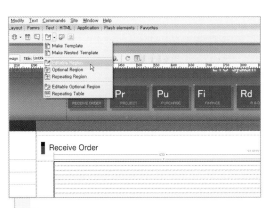

12 Insert a table into the right cell. The table should have 10 rows, 1 column, and a Table width of 630 pixels.

13 Select the table you just inserted and create an editable region by clicking the [Templates] icon (📄▾) and then selecting [Editable Region]. Text and other contents for the page will be inserted into this table, so you need to make the table editable.

14 In the New Editable Region dialog box, enter the name **insert-content**. Click [OK].

15 In the document window, the insert-content label indicates that the table is editable.

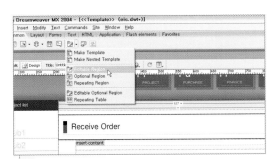

16 Since the header will be different on every page, select the header image and turn it into an editable region as well. Name this editable region **image-title**.

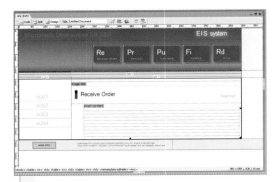

17 Editable areas are marked with a colored label. These labels push the editable area down slightly in Dreamweaver, but do not show up or affect placement in the Web browser. Select [File] - [Save] to save this template.

18 Now create five documents—**page1.htm**, **page2.htm**, **page3.htm**, **page4.htm**, and **page5.htm**—in the \Sample\ Chapter08\Section01 folder. This can be done easily by right-clicking in the Files panel and selecting [New File].

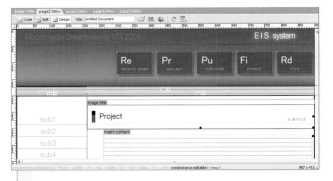

19 Open page1.htm. Go to the Assets panel and drag the eis template onto the document page. Do the same for page2.htm through page5.htm.

20 Select the Receive Order image in the page2.htm document. In the Properties Inspector, change the image to title2.gif in the Src field. The images folder contains five header images for each of the documents—apply title3.gif, title4.gif, and title5.gif to the corresponding documents.

## Vertical Cell Alignment

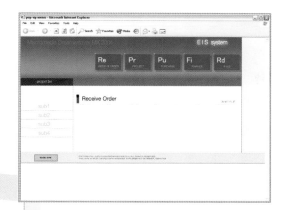

21 Looking at the final pages, you can see that the submenu on the left side of the page is now aligned vertically to the middle of the column. Previously, the submenu image was aligned to the top of the column. This is a common error. It occurs when the vertical alignment of the left column was set to default.

22 To fix the problem, open the template. Select the submenu image. Go to the Tag Selector and click on the <td> tag. In the Properties Inspector, set Vert (i.e., vertical alignment) to Top.

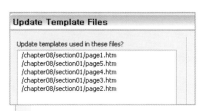

23 Save the changes using [Ctrl]-[S]. The Update Template Files dialog box will appear. Click [Update] to apply the changed template to the pages. Click [Close] when the Update Pages dialog box appears.

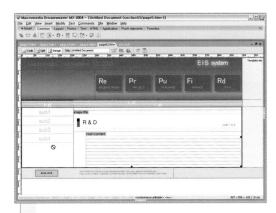

24 Looking at the Web pages, you will see that the submenu on the left is now aligned with the top of the column.

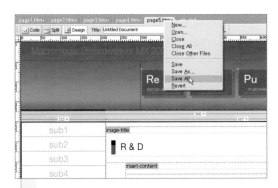

25 Because the Web pages have been changed, you need to save all of them again.

# Using Templates to Set Links

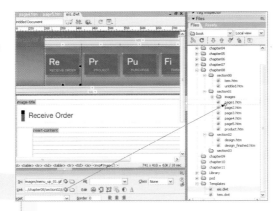

26 Next, let's link the five Web pages to the menu images by using a template. Select the Re menu image (menu_u_01.gif) in the template. In the Properties Inspector, drag the [Point to File] icon next to the Link field to the page1.htm file in the Files panel.

27 Add the respective page links for each of the remaining menu images in the order shown.

| Menu_up_01.gif | Menu_up_02.gif | Menu_up_03.gif | Menu_up_04.gif | Menu_up_05.gif |
| --- | --- | --- | --- | --- |
| Page1.htm | Page2.htm | Page3.htm | Page4.htm | Page5.htm |

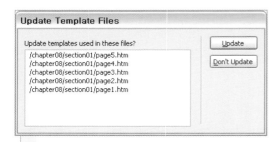

28 After setting up the links, save all the pages using [File] - [Save All] from the main menu. Since the template has been modified, you will be prompted to update all the files based on this template. Click [Update].

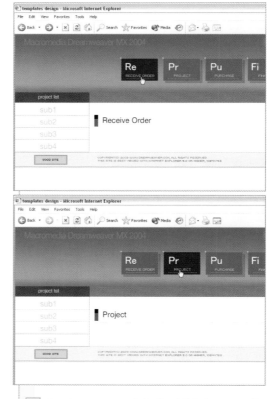

29 Preview your work in the Web browser. By using templates to set up links, you can easily add links without having to open all the pages and set up the links separately.

## Inserting Existing Elements into Editable Regions

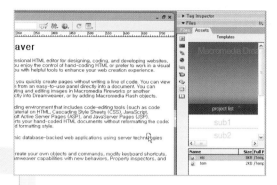

30 Open the page6.htm document, which contains some text. This text can be added directly to the eis template's editable region by dragging the template from the Assets panel onto the page.

31 The Inconsistent Region Names dialog box will appear. Select Document Body and choose insert-content in the Move Content to New Region option. This will move the text to the template's editable insert-content region. Click [OK].

32 By using templates, you can easily enter text or other elements into a page.

<< note

### Using Templates to Increase Team Efficiency

Templates can be used to aid the division of labor and increase the efficiency of a design team. The master designer will set up the template and only work on the template region. Using templates created by the master designer, the assistant designer can work on editing the contents of the page. A typist can create text for the pages by typing up a word processor document, and this can easily be imported into Dreamweaver.

# Removing Editable Regions

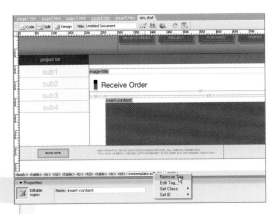

33 In order to remove editable regions, first select the region (in this case click on the insert-content label). Next, select [Modify] - [Templates] - [Remove Template Markup] or right-click on the <mmtemplate:editable> tag in the Tag Selector and select [Remove Tag]. As you can see, it is easier to use the Tag Selector to remove editable regions.

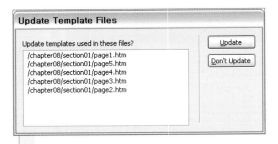

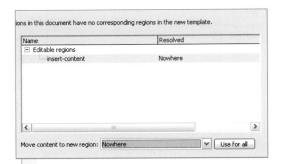

34 Click [File] - [Save] to save the template. When the Update Template Files dialog box appears, click [Update].

35 The Inconsistent Region Names dialog box will then appear. To remove all content such as tables, text, or images from the insert-content region, select insert-content and set the Move Content to New Region option to Nowhere. Click [OK]. Remember to save all the Web pages again since the template has been changed.

*Exercise*

# 2

# Using Templates and Style Sheets

In this exercise, we will use templates and style sheets together to create more sophisticated templates—in the form of nested templates and repeating regions.

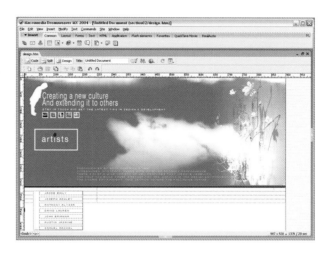

**Start File**

\Sample\Chapter08\Section02\design.htm

<< note

## Resource Files

Remember to copy the resource files on the CD-ROM to your local site before you start each exercise in this book.

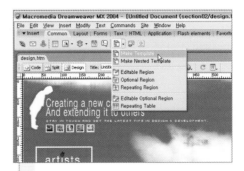

1 Open design.htm. In the Insert bar, click on the [Templates] icon ( ) and select [Make Template] to create a template from the design.htm document.

**249**

**2** Name the template **art**. Click [Save].

**3** If you look at the tab at the top of the Document window, you can see that the opened document is the art.dwt template and not the design.htm document any more. A template folder containing the art.dwt document will also be created in the site folder. If you cannot see the file, click the [Refresh] button (⟳) in the Files panel.

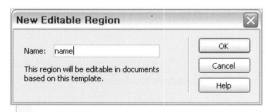

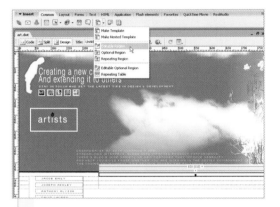

**4** Underneath the banner graphic is a table. Let's insert four tables into each of the four cells on the right of this table. Use the [Insert Table] icon (▦) to insert the tables, and in the Properties Inspector, specify the table as 650 pixels wide with 1 row and 1 column. Border thickness, Cell padding, and Cell spacing must all be set to 0.

**5** After inserting the four tables, you now have to convert them into editable regions. Select the first table in the Tag Selector, then click on the [Templates] button and select [Editable Region].

**6** Call the editable region **name**. Click [OK].

**7** Selecting the next three tables in turn, convert them into editable regions and name them **homepage**, **about**, and **insert,** respectively.

# Adding Style Sheets

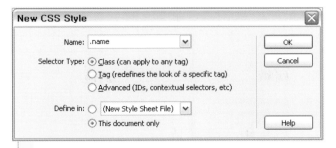

8  Let's add style sheets to the editable regions. Right-click on the name table and select [CSS Styles] - [New]. Call the new style **.name** and choose [This document only] under the Define In option. Click [OK].

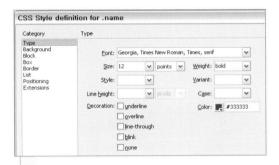

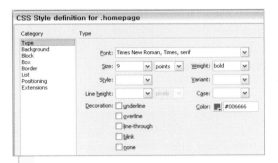

9  In the CSS Style definition dialog box for .name, check that the Type category is selected. Choose [Georgia, Times New Roman, Times, serif] under the font option. Set the font size to 12 pixels, weight to bold, and color to #333333. Click OK. Right-click on the name table and select [CSS Styles] - [name] to apply the style. Notice that the bottom name label is displayed in the style you just added. Delete this bottom label as it will appear in the final page.

10  Now, add a new style, .homepage, to the homepage table. In the CSS Style definition dialog box, set its type properties to [Times New Roman, Times, serif], 9 points, bold, and color #006666. Click [OK]. Next, apply the style on the table and delete the bottom label.

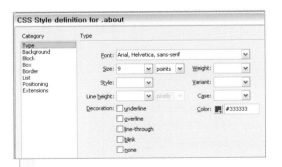

11  Insert a new style, .about, in the .about table. In the CSS Style definition dialog box, set its type properties to [Arial, Helvetica, sans-serif], 9 points, and color #333333. Click [OK]. Next, apply the style on the table and delete the bottom label.

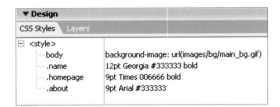

| <style> | |
|---|---|
| body | background-image: url(images/bg/main_bg.gif) |
| .name | 12pt Georgia #333333 bold |
| .homepage | 9pt Times 006666 bold |
| .about | 9pt Arial #333333 |

**12** Applying a style to a template will apply the style to all documents that use the template. In the Design panel, click on the CSS Styles tab and check that the styles have been created. Click [File] - [Save] to save the template. For more information about style sheets, see Chapter 3.

**13** Open one of the seven files that are filled with text (Such as 01_Jacob_emily.htm). Go to the Assets panel and drag the art template onto the page.

&lt;&lt; note

## Using Arrow Keys

Although the name, homepage, and about tables have been converted into editable regions, since we did so by selecting the <td> tag instead of inserting a table into the cell, the results will be slightly different. Editable regions can be specified by selecting <table> or <td>. The results are largely the same, the main difference being in the scope of the editable region itself.

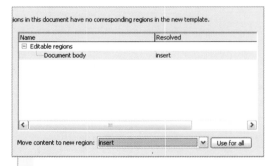

**14** In the Inconsistent Region Names dialog box, select Document body and set the [Move Content to New Region] option to insert. Click [OK].

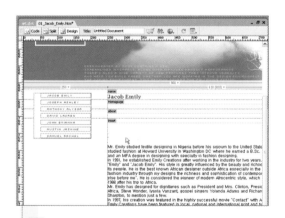

**15** All of the text has now been inserted into the insert editable region. Select each line of text and move it to the proper location—name, homepage, and about.

<< note

## Tidying Up Your Workspace

In the Inconsistent Region Names dialog box, if you choose to move the text to one of the editable regions where a style has been applied, you will find that the style will not be applied automatically to the text. The insert region is needed as sort of a holding area for the text until it is moved to an editable region that has a style. You need to physically move the text into a region with a style in order for the style to take effect.

16 The above image shows the text placement after all the text has been moved. Now open all the other six documents containing text. Apply the art template, slot the text into the different editable regions, and then save your work. Check that all empty spaces and lines from the insert editable region are removed so that the insert table returns to its original size.

17 Preview your work in the Web browser. You will notice that the name, homepage address, and designer's introduction are too close together. Let's leave it as it is for now.

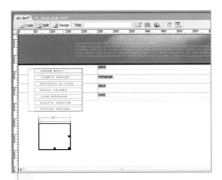

18 Select the [Layout] category of the Insert bar and click on the [Draw Layer] button (🗔). Create a new layer and move it down as shown. Click inside the layer and click the [Table] button (🖽) to insert a table into the layer. Set the table properties to width = 100 pixels, rows = 1 and columns = 1. In the Properties Inspector, set the table height to 83 pixels.

19 Next, select the [Common] category of the Insert bar and click the [Template] button (📄▾) to make the table an editable region. Name the region **image**. Click [File] - [Save] to save and update the template.

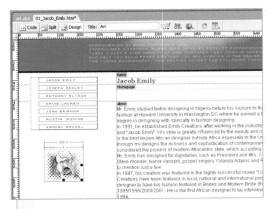

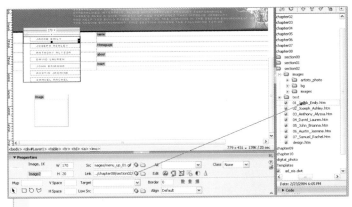

**20** Insert the designers' photos from the \Sample\Chapter08\Section02\images\artists_ photo folder into the image region of each of the seven files. The file names are numbered and should be easy to find.

**21** Select the menu images of the artists' names on the left and set up the links one by one.

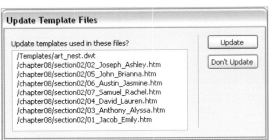

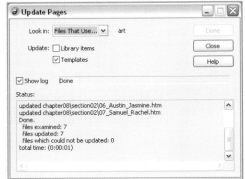

**22** After setting up the links, select [File] - [Save] to save and update the template.

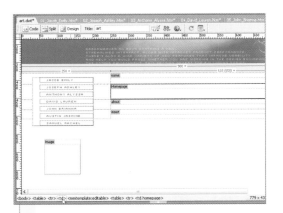

**23** Hit [F12] to preview your work in the Web browser. Check if the links work. You can see that the name and homepage address are too close together.

**24** Select the name or homepage editable regions. In the Tag Selector, select the <td> tag. This selects the cell containing the region. Let's adjust the height of the name and homepage cells. Set the height of the name cell to 30 pixels and the homepage cell to 40 pixels. When you are done, save and update your template.

25 Here is what a preview of the page looks like. By making the cells that contain the name and homepage address larger, the information is clearer and easier to read.

# Making Nested Templates

<< note

## Information about Nested Templates

Nested templates are sub-templates added to the master template (i.e., a template-within-a-template). You can make nested templates by saving them in the documents that use the original template. In other words, nested templates cannot be saved if the template document is open.

26 Open one of the seven files. Click the [Templates] button (📄·) and select [Make Nested Templates].

27 Call the template **art_nest**. Click [Save].

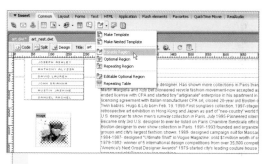

28 From the tabs at the top of the Document window, you will see that the art_nest.dwt template file has been created. At the top-right corner of the art_nest template, you will see a yellow [Template:art] label. This means that this nested template is made from the art.dwt template. Making any changes to the art template will also affect the art_nest.dw template.

29 In a page made using nested templates, you can create another editable region inside the editable region. Click on the insert cell and then click on the [Templates] button (  ) and select [Editable Region].

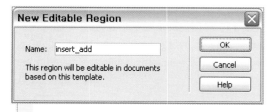

30 Name the region **insert_add** and press [OK].

31 When an editable region is created inside the editable region of a nested template, a yellow label will appear.

# Repeating Regions

## Uses for Repeating Regions

Repeating regions come in handy when entering repeating elements inside templates.

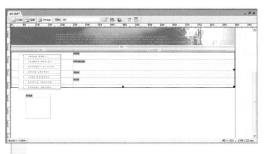

32 Select the table in the art.dwt file as shown here and enter 5 in the Rows option in the Properties Inspector.

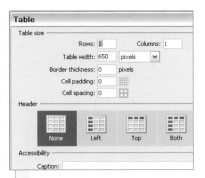

33 Insert another table inside the new row. Set the properties of the table to 1 row, 1 column, and 650 pixels. Set everything else to 0. Click [OK].

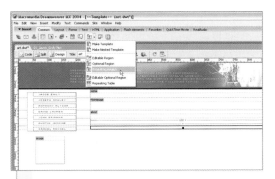

34 Select the table and click on the [Templates] button ( ) and select [Repeating Region].

35 Name the repeating region **repeat**. Click OK.

36 You will see the [Repeat: repeat] label appear in light green. Save your work. It is good to get in the habit of saving your templates immediately after making changes, and then applying the update.

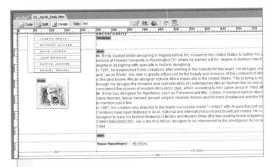

37 Open a document that uses the template. A +/- and an up/down menu will appear in the repeating region. If there is an element that needs to be repeated, simply press the [+] button to increase the number of tables. Conversely, in order to remove repeating regions, select the table and press the [-] button. However, in this case, since you have yet to set up the regions as editable regions, these buttons will not work.

38 In order to activate the [-] button (to delete regions), you need to change the repeating region to an editable region. Go back to the template and select the <td> tag for the repeating region in the Tag Selector. Click on the [Templates] button and select [Editable Region]. Make sure you select the correct tag or you may get a message saying the region is already editable.

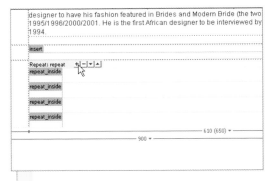

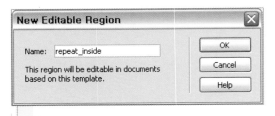

39 Call the editable region **repeat_inside**.

40 Now that the regions are set up as editable regions, you can use the +/- buttons to manage the repeating regions. In the document, use the [Add] button (+) to create repeating regions, and then remove them with the [Remove] button (-) .

# Using the Replace Command to Update Links

When you change folder names or move files in Dreamweaver, they are automatically updated. But if folder names are changed outside the program, for example if another person changes the name of your folder in Windows Explorer, then Dreamweaver and the Web browser will not recognize the new paths and the page will not appear. This can often happen if a number of people are working on the same project. In such instances, you need to rework the source code using the Replace command.

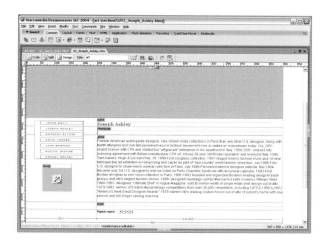

1 In Dreamweaver, you use the Files panel to change the name of an image folder.

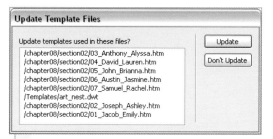

2 When folder names are changed in Dreamweaver, the Update Files dialog box will appear and the path will be updated automatically.

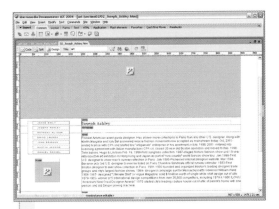

3 For this exercise, go to Windows Explorer and locate the resource files which you used in the last exercise. Change the artists_photo folder to artists_photo_photo and the bg folder to bg_img.

4 If you open one of the Web pages you designed in the previous exercise, you will find that the image links are broken. The links will be broken in the template, as well.

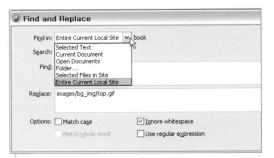

5 In the art.dwt template, select the image at the top and click on the [Split] button to show both Design and Code Views. The image you selected is found in the bg_img folder which was previously named the bg folder. Select the image and note the position of the image in the source code.

6 Press [Ctrl]-[F] to open the Find and Replace dialog box. The important thing to remember is that you must use the Find in option with caution. Selecting [Enter Current Local Site] allows you to change the source code for all documents in the current site at one time. Choose the option that you need.

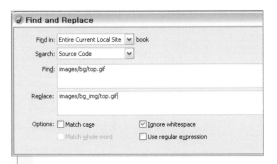

7 Enter the Find and Replace information. Since we changed the bg folder to bg_img, enter the following and select [Replace All].

## Find and Replace in Template Documents

When working with template documents, set the Find in option to [Selected Files in Site]. Make sure the template is selected in the Files panel. This is because if the template path is modified, the path of the documents that use the template will also change automatically. You must save the template after making the changes to update the code of the respective documents.

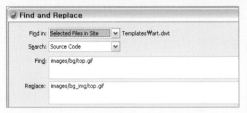

8 When the Replace command is used to change the source code, Dreamweaver will show you the results of the change in the Search window. In this case, one change has been made.

9 When you save the template, the respective documents will be updated accordingly.

10 Although you have updated the link to the background image, you still need to update the link to the designers' photographs. Open one of the designer's files, in this case 03_carole_guevin.htm, and click on the photo image.

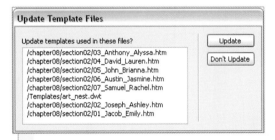

11 Set Find in to [Enter Current Local Site], enter the Find and Replace paths and then select [Replace All].

12 The Search window shows that the new path has been updated for all the documents that use it.

**Chapter** 9

# Inserting Multimedia Elements into Web Pages

In this chapter, you will learn how to use Dreamweaver MX 2004 to insert media files and interactivity into your Web pages. Multimedia files are usually created in other programs, such as Flash, before they are inserted into a Web page. However, you can create simple Flash buttons and text directly in Dreamweaver. In this chapter, you will use multimedia files to create the sort of effects seen in online lecture pages, music video pages, and Internet broadcasting sites.

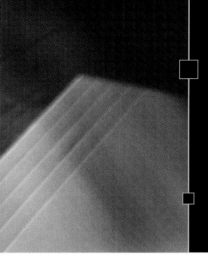

# The Basics of Working with Multimedia Elements

There are many types of multimedia content that can be inserted into Web pages. In this section, you will look at the different types of multimedia files, with an emphasis on working with common elements such as Flash files and QuickTime movies.

## Plug-Ins and ActiveX Controls

Web browsers by themselves cannot display and handle multimedia files. When a browser detects a file that it cannot cope with, it will find and launch an application on your computer that can deal with the file. For example, it may launch a word processor such as Microsoft Word to open a document file.

Alternatively, it may look for auxiliary programs that extend its ability to play the file. To enable their browsers to manage a variety of multimedia content, Netscape developed plug-in technology. Microsoft, on the other hand, uses ActiveX controls to achieve the same result. These auxiliary programs add functionality to Web browsers. For instance, if a page contains a Flash file, the web browser will use the Flash Player plug-in or equivalent ActiveX control to display the file correctly. Media content is inserted into Web pages using the <embed> tag (plug-ins) or <object> tag (ActiveX).

## Multimedia File Formats Supported by Web Browsers

Flash, Shockwave, and QuickTime movies–as well as other multimedia file formats–can all be added to a Dreamweaver page. Let's have a look at each of them:

### Flash Files

Flash files (FLA) are the source files for a Flash project (made using the Flash program). They can only be opened in the Flash program and must be exported as SWF or SWT files before they can be used by Dreamweaver or the Web browser.

The Flash SWF file is a compressed version of the Flash (FLA) file and is optimized for viewing in the Web browser. Although the SWF file can be played in the Web browser and previewed in Dreamweaver, it cannot be edited. SWF files are normally used to make Flash buttons and Flash text.

The Flash template file (SWT) allows you to edit or change the information in a Flash movie. This file is used to make Flash button objects, and user-defined SWF files can insert desired text or links into the Web page. Flash template files can be found in the Dreamweaver/Configuration/Flash Objects/Flash Buttons folder and the Flash Text folder.

The Flash elements file (SWC) is a type of Flash SWF file used to make colorful Internet application programs. Flash elements also contain parameters which can be defined by the user. By modifying these parameters, you can execute the features of other application programs.

## Other File Formats

- **AIFF** (Audio Interchange File Format) files (.aif), like WAV files, are high-quality format files that can be used in many browsers without the need for plug-ins. AIFF is a digital audio file format from Apple that is used on the Macintosh. They can be recorded directly using CDs, cassette tapes, or a microphone, but their large size limits the length of sound clips for Web use.

- **ASF** (Advanced Streaming Format) is the newest standard in media streaming. ASF, a type of streaming file, is also the recording format used by Microsoft.

- **AVI** (Audio Video Interleaved) refers to both the file format that supports digital video in Windows, and the name given to the Windows video product that was introduced at the 1992 COMDEX exhibition. AVI was first used by Microsoft in an attempt to play videos in Windows. AVI was developed to solve the problems of full-motion video support for multimedia technology, and is defined as an audio/video-interleave format compression software for MPC multimedia systems.

- **MIDI** (Musical Instrument Digital Interface) files (.midi or .mid) are electronic music files. Many browsers support the MIDI file format without the need for a plug-in, and MIDI files compress long sound clips into small files. The sound quality of MIDI files is very good, but it is dependent on the user's sound card. MIDI files are not recorded from other sources; they are created using computer software on machines with the appropriate hardware.

- **MP3** (Motion Picture Experts Group Audio or MPEG-Audio Layer-3) files (.mp3) use a compressed file format that allows high-quality sound in very small files. The sound quality of MP3 files is so good that if you record and compress the sound properly, you can achieve near-CD quality. MP3 files use streaming technology, which means that visitors can listen to the sound without having to wait for the file to finish downloading. However, MP3 files are larger than Real Audio files and downloading can be quite slow using a regular dial-up modem. To play MP3 files, you need the QuickTime Player, Windows Media Player, or RealPlayer plug-ins–or you will need to install application programs that play this format.

- **MPEG** (Moving Picture Expert Group) was first established in 1988 and is a compression/dissolution standard for movies. Unlike JPEG, which was designed to compress still images, MPEG strives to improve data transmission of movies through compression and coding of the data. There are different types of MPEG: MPEG-1 offers VCR quality and MPEG-2 offers high-resolution, digital video support. The latest standard, MPEG-4, supports object-by-object encoding for all types of multimedia data, and is the international multimedia standard for state-of-the-art Internet, digital TV, DVD, and mobile communication.

- **QuickTime** (.qt, .qtm, .mov) files are combined audio/video file formats developed by Apple Computer. QuickTime is included in Apple Macintosh operating systems and can be used in most Macintosh application programs used for audio, video, and animation. Although QuickTime can also be played on the PC, you will need a special QuickTime player to do so. QuickTime supports Cinepak, JPEG, MPEG, and most other encoding formats.

- **Real Audio** (.ra, .ram, .rpm) file formats have high compression rates, which make them smaller than MP3 files, with an acceptable download time for a complete song. On regular Web servers, these files use streaming technology, which means that visitors can listen to the sound while it is downloading. RealPlayer files require the download and installation of application programs or plug-ins to play the format.

- **WAV** (Waveform Extension) files (.wav) also have good sound quality and are supported by many browsers without the need for plug-ins. WAV files can be created directly from CDs, cassette tapes, or a microphone. However, WAV files tend to be large, which limits the length of sound clips for use in the Web browser.

- **WMA** (Windows Media Audio) files (.wma) use voice compression, and are part of Microsoft's Windows Media Technologies 4.0. This file format supports streaming technology and has a high compression rate that can compress audio files to half the size of regular MP3 files. This file format also contains the Windows Media Rights Manager, which helps protect copyrights. WMA files can be played using the Windows Media Player.

- **WMV** (Windows Media Video), Microsoft's Windows media file, contains both audio and video–unlike WMA, which only contains audio files. Of all the video file formats available now, WMV has the best compression, making it one of the more widely used formats today.

# Inserting Flash Files

Since both Flash and Dreamweaver are Macromedia products, Macromedia has made it easy to insert Flash movies in Dreamweaver. And since Flash is also a popular program for creating animations for the Internet, let's see how you can insert Flash movies into your Web pages.

1. To insert a Flash file, simply go to the Insert bar, select the [Common] category, click the [Media] button ( ), and select [Flash] ( ).

2. Select the Flash file and press [OK] to insert it into the page.

266

3. Click on the Flash file, go to the Properties Inspector, and press the [Play] button () to preview the Flash movie.

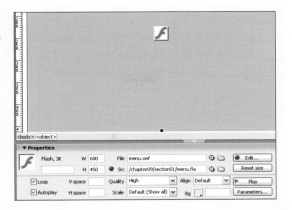

<< tip

## Insertion by Drag-and-Drop

You can also drag-and-drop the SWF file from the File panel onto the page. In addition to being easier, this method also inserts the file path of the original file automatically into the Properties Inspector. If you have Flash MX installed on your computer, press the [Edit] button (  Edit...  ) to edit the original source.

## Creating Flash Buttons

You can also create Flash buttons directly in Dreamweaver without having to use the Flash program.

1. Select the [Common] category of the Insert bar, then click on the [Media] button ( ● · ) and select [Flash Button] ( Flash Button ) to insert a pre-made Flash button. Flash buttons come with Dreamweaver even if you do not have the Flash program.

2. Select the style of button you want, and in the Button Text field, type in the text that will appear on the button in the Web browser. Then, in the Save As field, type in the name for your button file. You can also enter the Flash link address.

3. Press [OK]. This will create the button1.swf file in the Files panel.

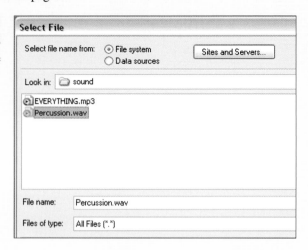

## Inserting Sound

A good choice of background music can enhance your Web site, but a bad choice can put off some users. In this section, let's learn to insert sound files into your Web pages.

1. From the Insert bar, select the [Common] category, click on the [Media] button ( ), and select [Plugin] ( Plugin ). Select the music file from the Sound folder.

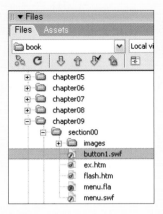

2. When the source code has been entered, go to Code View.

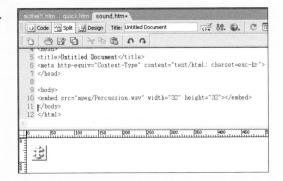

3. Set both the height and width to 1 so that the music file will take up hardly any space on the page. Option values allow you to setup the sound in different ways. Source coding the options is done in Code View.

```
5  <title>Untitled Document</title>
6  <meta http-equiv="Content-Type" content="text/html; charset=euc-kr">
7  </head>
8
9  <body>
10 <embed src="mpeg/Percussion.wav" width="1" height="1" autostart="true" loop="true" hidden="false" ></embed>
11 </body>
12 </html>
13
```

<< tip

**Shortcut to Stop Background Music**

Press the [Esc] key to stop background music from playing.

## Inserting QuickTime Files

QuickTime is a video file format developed by Apple. To be able to insert QuickTime files, you need to first install the Insert_QuickTime.mxp extension using the Extension Manager program.

1. After installing the extension, restart Dreamweaver and you will see that the QuickTime Movie menu is added to the Insert bar. Click on the [QuickTime Movie] menu to insert a QuickTime file.

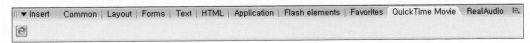

2. Select the \Sample\Chapter09\Section00\mpeg\reel.mov file and press [OK].

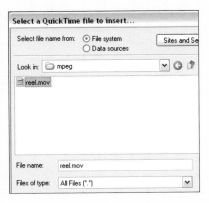

**269**

3. After inserting the QuickTime file and selecting the file in step 2, you will see some complicated looking properties, such as ClassID and Base. Preview the results. If the player is not activated, go to http://www.apple.com/quicktime and download the latest version of QuickTime.

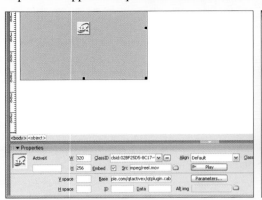 

**When QuickTime movies are inserted and the code is viewed, you will see the following tags:**

**classid**: You can think of this as the name of the ActiveX control. When you visit a site that uses ActiveX, a dialog box will pop up asking you to install an ActiveX control if it is not already installed. If you respond yes, an ActiveX control will automatically be installed on your computer. When you do this, it will be added to the registry and the classid value will call the ActiveX control to play the file in the Web browser.

**codebase**: This is the URL that generates the absolute path when the object is set up using the relative path. Here, codebase tells you the position of the compressed QuickTime player install file.

```
<object classid = "clsid:02BF25D5-8C17-4B23-BC80-D3488ABDDC6B" codebase =
"http://www.apple.com/qtactivex/qtplugin.cab" width="320" height="256">

   <param name="autoplay" value="true">

   <param name="controller" value="true">

   <param name="pluginspage" value="http://www.apple.com/quicktime/download/
   indext.htm">

   <param name="target" value="myself">

   <param name="type" value="video/quicktime">

   <param name="src" value="mpeg/reel.mov">

   <embed  src="mpeg/reel.mov"  width="320"  height="256"  autoplay="true"
   controller="true" border="0" pluginspage="http://www.apple.com/quicktime
   /download/indext.htm" target="myself"></embed>

</object>
```

## Inserting Video Files

Video files come in two main varieties–those that are streamed and play in the Web browser while they are downloading from the Internet, and those that need to be downloaded fully onto your computer before they can be played. For streaming files, WMV files work best. WMV is a compressed file format developed by Microsoft. The latest version is version 9 and this file format offers different resolution types to fit your Internet connection speed.

Generally, AVI, MPEG, ASF, and WMV files are all entered using the ActiveX menu. We usually recommend WMV files because they have the highest compression and best resolution of all the streaming files.

Whereas you needed to install an extension for inserting QuickTime files into Dreamweaver, Dreamweaver does not have a menu for the addition of WMV files. You first need to go to ActiveX and then edit the parameter codes to complete the video file setup.

1. From the Insert bar, select the [Common] category, click on the [Media] button (  ), and select [ActiveX].

2. Set the width to 352 and height to 285, and select classid: 22D6F312-B0F6-11D0-94AB-0080C74C7E95 from the Properties Inspector. If this is not included in the list, you can enter it directly in the ClassID field or by selecting Code View and entering it manually into the code. Enter **http://activex.microsoft.com/activex/ controls/mplayer/en/nsmp2inf.cab#Version=5,1,52,701** in the Base field.

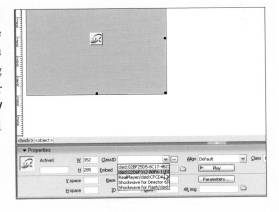

3. In Code View, you can see that the file has been entered.

```
 7  </head>
 8
 9  <body>
10    <p>
11      <object classid="clsid:22D6F312-B0F6-11D0-94AB-0080C74C7E95" codebase=
"http://activex.microsoft.com/activex/controls/mplayer/en/nsmp2inf.cab#Version=5,1,52,701" width="352" height="285" id="MediaPlayer">
12      </object>
13    </p>
14    <p> </p>
15  </body>
16  </html>
```

4. In the Properties Inspector, click on the [Parameters...] icon and enter the information shown in the screenshot to the right.

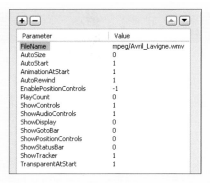

| Parameter | Value |
|---|---|
| FileName | mpeg/Avril_Lavigne.wmv |
| AutoSize | 0 |
| AutoStart | 1 |
| AnimationAtStart | 1 |
| AutoRewind | 1 |
| EnablePositionControls | -1 |
| PlayCount | 0 |
| ShowControls | 1 |
| ShowAudioControls | 1 |
| ShowDisplay | 0 |
| ShowGotoBar | 0 |
| ShowPositionControls | 0 |
| ShowStatusBar | 0 |
| ShowTracker | 1 |
| TransparentAtStart | 1 |

5. You can also type in the properties directly in Code View. This is the more convenient method because Code View comes with code hints that help reduce potential errors.

```
9  <body>
10 <object  classid="clsid:22D6F312-B0F6-11D0-94AB-0080C74C7E95"
11     CODEBASE="http://activex.microsoft.com/activex/controls/mplayer/en/nsmp2inf.cab#Version=5,1,52,701"
12     TYPE="application/x-oleobject"  width="352" height="285" align="top" standby="Loading Microsoft?Windows?Media Player components..."
13     <param name="FileName"  value="mpeg/Avril_Lavigne.wmv">
14     <param name="AutoSize" value="0">
15     <param name="AutoStart" value="1">
16     <param name="AnimationAtStart" value="1">
17     <param name="AutoRewind" value="1">
18     <param name="EnablePositionControls" value="-1">
19     <param name="PlayCount" value="0">
20     <param name="ShowControls" value="1">
21     <param name="ShowAudioControls" value="1">
22     <param name="ShowDisplay" value="0">
23     <param name="ShowGotoBar" value="0">
24     <param name="ShowPositionControls" value="0">
25     <param name="ShowStatusBar" value="0">
26     <param name="ShowTracker" value="1">
27     <param name="TransparentAtStart" value="1">
28 </object>
29 </body>
30 </html>
```

6. Preview your work in the browser to see that the WMV file plays properly.

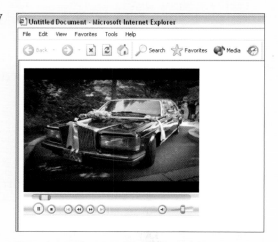

## A Closer Look at Parameters

Parameters allow you to give movie files diverse properties.

**<param name="ClickToPlay" value="0">**: When set to 1, clicking the mouse will repeat, play, or pause the file.

**<param name="Enabled" value="1">**: When set to 1, you can use the buttons. When set to 0, buttons are disabled.

**<param name="EnableTracker" value="1">**: When set to 0, the slide bar in the tracker is disabled.

**<param name="EnableContextMenu" value="0">**: When set to 1, you can right-click the mouse and use the shortcut menu.

**<param name="ShowCaptioning" value="1">**: When set to 1, the caption window will be visible.

**<param name="Mute" value="1">**: When set to 1, sound will not play.

**<param name="FileName" value="mpeg/my_music.wmv">**: Type in the name of the file to play inside the quotes that follow "value". You can play AVI, MPEG, WMV, and ASF files.

**<param name="AutoSize" value="0">**: When set to 0, the size is fixed. When set to 1, sizing occurs automatically.

**<param name="AutoStart" value="1">**: When set to 1, framing occurs automatically. When set to 0, you must use the buttons.

**<param name="AnimationAtStart" value="1">**: When set to 1, the animation logo will move as the video file is buffered.

**<param name="AutoRewind" value="1">**: When set to 1, rewind occurs automatically.

**<param name="PlayCount" value="0">**: Type in how many times the file will be played.

**<param name="ShowControls" value="1">**: When set to 1, the control panel will be visible.

**<param name="ShowAudioControls" value="1">**: When set to 1, the volume control panel will be visible.

**<param name="ShowDisplay" value="0">**: When set to 1, file information (name, author, copyright) will be displayed.

**<param name="ShowGotoBar" value="0">**: When set to 1, goto bar will be visible.

**<param name="ShowPositionControls" value="0">**: Displays position controls (-1 = true, 0 = false).

**<param name="ShowStatusBar" value="0">**: When set to 1, displays status bar at the bottom.

**<param name="ShowTracker" value="1">**: When set to 1, shows status of the playing track.

**<param name="TransparentAtStart" value="1">**: When set to 1, file is transparent at start.

# Exercise 1

## Making an Online Lecture Page

Given the fact that both Flash and Dreamweaver are the leading products from Macromedia, it comes as no surprise that it is so easy to insert Flash movies in Dreamweaver. Although there are many other video file formats available on the market, these files are more difficult to control in Dreamweaver. Since you can open all types of media files in Flash, it is recommended that you create and output these files using Flash before bringing them into Dreamweaver. In this exercise, you will learn to create button controls for a Flash movie.

**Start File**

○— \Sample\Chapter09\Section01\cyber.htm

**Final File**

○— \Sample\Chapter09\Section01\cyber_finished.htm

<< note

### Resource Files

Remember to copy the resource files on the CD-ROM to your local site before you start each exercise in this book.

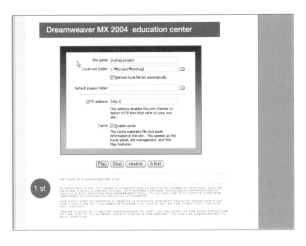

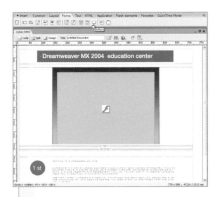

1 Open cyber.htm. You will notice that the start file is a document that contains a Flash file. You are going to insert four buttons (Play, Stop, Rewind, Go to 1) at the bottom of the Flash file. Move the mouse cursor to the table row below the Flash File. In the Insert bar, select the [Forms] category and click on the [Button] icon (▢).

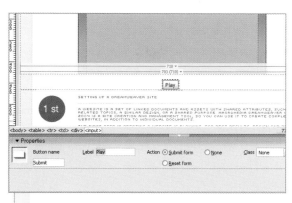

**Dreamweaver**

⚠ Add form tag?

☐ Don't show me this message again

[Yes] [No]

2 | A dialog box will appear asking if you would like to insert form tags. Since you are only going to be making buttons, you do not need to add form tags. Select [No].

3 | In the Properties Inspector, set the Label to **Play**.

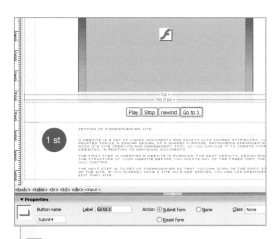

4 | Repeat the steps to add and label three more buttons. Label the buttons as **Stop**, **Rewind**, and **Go to 1** respectively.

5 | With the Play button selected, go to the Tag Inspector, select the [Behaviors] tab, and click the [Add Behavior] icon ( +, ). Select [Control Shockwave or Flash] from the list of behaviors.

<< note

## The Movie is Not Found

If you find that the movie you want to control is not listed in the Movie option in the Control Shockwave or Flash dialog box, it is most likely because the movie was not given a name. To fix the problem, all you need to do is to select the Flash file and, in the Properties Inspector, give it a name. In this exercise, for example, the Flash movie is named edu.

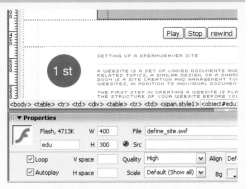

6 In the Control Shockwave or Flash dialog box, set the Action to Play. Click [OK].

7 Similarly, select the Stop button in the Document window, and in the Tag Inspector, click on the [Behaviors] tab and the [Add Behavior] icon ( + ). Then select [Control Shockwave or Flash] from the list of behaviors. Set the Action to Stop and click [OK].

8 Repeat step 7 to give the Rewind button the Rewind action.

9 For the Go to 1 button, repeat step 7 but set the action to [Go to frame] and insert the value as 1. This tells the program to move to frame 1 of the Flash file. Right now, the Go to 1 button acts just like the Rewind button; both buttons will take you back to the beginning of the movie. However, the advantage of the [Go to frame] option is that you can designate which frame the movie will jump to.

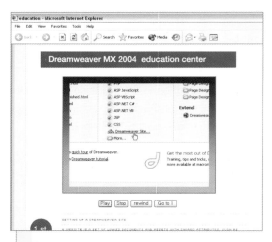

10 Press [F12] to preview the movie in the Web browser and check that the buttons work properly.

# Inserting a RealVideo File

RealVideo is a streaming video technology for the Web. To insert a RealVideo or a RealAudio file, which uses streaming audio technology, you need to install the RealSystem extension for Dreamweaver which will make the process a lot simpler. The RealVideo file can be played on a Web browser using the RealOne media player (formerly RealPlayer) plug-in. To be able to preview the video in your Web browser, you need to have the RealOne media player. You can download this for free from the www.real.com Web site.

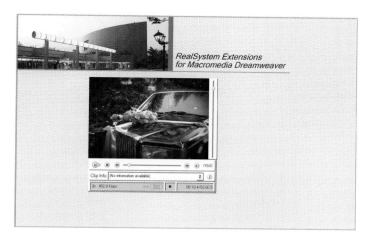

**Start File**
\Sample\Chapter09\Section02\real.htm

**Final File**
\Sample\Chapter09\Section02\real_finished.htm

**Extension File**
MX219592_RealNetworks.mxp

MX219592_RealNetworks.mxp
MXP File
54 KB

1 Install the extension, MX219592_ RealNetworks.mxp by double-clicking on the file in the Windows Explorer. This extension makes it easier to insert RealMedia files. Once the extension has been installed, restart Dreamweaver in order to use the extension.

<< note

### Resource Files

Remember to copy the resource files on the CD-ROM to your local site before you start each exercise in this book.

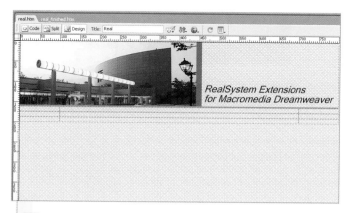

2 Open real.htm. Place the cursor in the table's middle cell.

Download the extension file from the Macromedia Web site. See page 9 for instructions for downloading extensions.

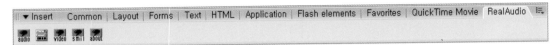

3 From the Insert bar, select the [RealAudio] menu and click on the RealVideo icon (📷).

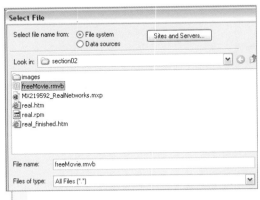

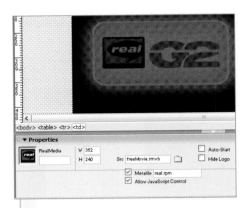

4 In the Select File dialog box, select the video file, freeMovie.rmvb. Click [OK].

5 In the Properties Inspector, check the Auto-Start and Hide Logo options. Set the width of the movie to 352 pixels and height to 240 pixels.

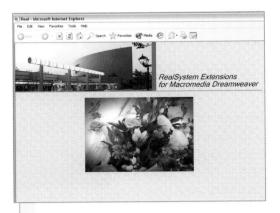

6 Then place the cursor anywhere in the cell with the video clip and align the video to center.

7 Preview your work in the Web browser by pressing [F12]. The movie plays in the browser, but, as you can see, a control panel is still required.

8 Move the cursor to the table cell directly below the video file and click the RealMedia Control icon (▦) from the Insert bar's [RealAudio] menu.

9 From the RealMedia Control dialog box, select Basic Control, which is the most basic control panel, and click [OK].

10 Since the width of the movie screen is 352 pixels, select the control bar and set the W value to 352. This will line up the control bar with the movie screen.

11 Then, place the cursor in the cell with the control panel and set the alignment to center.

12 Press [F12] to preview your work in the Web browser. Notice that the movie now has a control bar that includes a Play button and displays information on the file and connection speed.

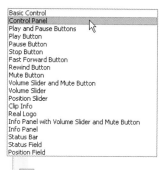

13 Although both the Basic Control and Control Panel are commonly used, the more common of the two is the Control Panel. Let's replace the Basic Control you inserted with the Control Panel. Select and delete the Basic Control from the Document window and add the Control Panel. If you can't remember how to do this, refer to steps 8 and 9.

14 The Control Panel will be added below the movie and the volume slider will be added on the right-hand side.

15 Preview your work by pressing [F12] in the Web browser. Make sure that the Play button and the volume slider work properly.

```
31  <tr>
32    <td width="100"> </td>
33    <td width="600">        <div align="center">
34      <object id="RVOCX" classid="CLSID:CFCDAA03-8BE4-11cf-B84B-0020AFBBCCFA" width="352" height="240">
35        <param name="SRC" value="real.rpm">
36        <param name="CONTROLS" value="ImageWindow">
37        <param name="CONSOLE" value="cons">
38        <embed src="real.rpm" type="audio/x-pn-realaudio-plugin" width="352" height="240" controls="ImageWindow" console="cons"> </embe
39      </object>
40      <object id=RVOCX classid="CLSID:CFCDAA03-8BE4-11CF-B84B-0020AFBBCCFA" width="26" height="240" >
41        <param name="SRC" value="real.rpm">
42        <param name="CONTROLS" value="VolumeSlider">
43        <param name="CONSOLE" value="cons">
44        <embed src="real.rpm" type="audio/x-pn-realaudio-plugin" width="26" height="240" controls="VolumeSlider" console="cons" > </e
45      </object>
46  </div></td>
47    <td width="100"> </td>
48  </tr>
49  <tr>
50    <td width="100"> </td>
51    <td width="600">        <div align="center">
52      <object id=RVOCX classid="CLSID:CFCDAA03-8BE4-11CF-B84B-0020AFBBCCFA" width="352" height="100" >
53        <param name="SRC" value="real.rpm">
54        <param name="CONTROLS" value="All">
55        <param name="CONSOLE" value="cons">
56        <embed src="real.rpm" type="audio/x-pn-realaudio-plugin" width="352" height="100" controls="All" console="cons" > </embed>
57      </object>
58    </div></td>
59    <td width="100"> </td>
60  </tr>
61  </table>
62  <p> 
63    </p>
```

16 If you check your work in Code View, you can see that the movie is inserted into the Web page using the <object> tag and that the code looks quite complex. Without the benefit of the extension you installed earlier, you would have had to enter this complex-looking code by hand.

# Making a Music Video Page

In this section, you will learn to insert a movie as an ActiveX object, setting the parameters for this object to control such actions as whether the movie will start automatically. You will add Play, Stop, and Pause button functions by entering some JavaScript into the page.

> **Start File**
> • \Sample\Chapter09\Section03\music.htm

> **Final File**
> • \Sample\Chapter09\Section03\music_finished.htm

<< note

**Resource Files**

Remember to copy the resource files on the CD-ROM to your local site before you start each exercise in this book.

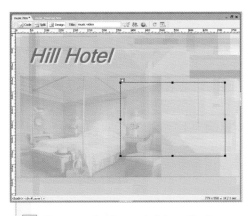

1 Open music.htm and click on the layer.

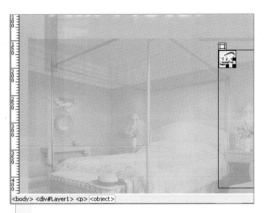

<body> <div#Layer1> <p> <object>

2 In the Insert bar, select the [Common] category and click on the [Media] button (⊕ ·). Select [Active X].

3 You can see from the Tag Selector that the <object> tag has been added to the page. Next, you will need to edit the object's properties.

4 With the ActiveX object selected in the Document window, go to the Properties Inspector. Set the ActiveX object's width to 352 pixels and height to 240 pixels, then select clsid:22D6F312-B0F6-11D0-94AB-0080C74C7E95 in the ClassID option. If this ClassID is not on the list, you can enter it directly into the textbox for ClassID. The Base value should be http://activex.microsoft.com/activex/controls/mplayer/en/nsmp2inf.cab#Version=5,1,52,701. Click on the [Parameters] button in the Properties Inspector.

5 In the Parameters dialog box, type in the parameter FileName and set its value to freeMovie.wmv. To enter the next parameter, click the [+] button. Next, enter the parameter ShowStatusBar and set its value to 0 (0 indicates "no" and 1 indicates "yes"). This means that the status bar will not be shown. Then enter the AutoStart parameter and set a value of 1. Enter the ShowControls, AllowChangeDisplaySize, and DisplaySize parameters and set all their values to 0. Check that you've entered all the names and values correctly. Click [OK].

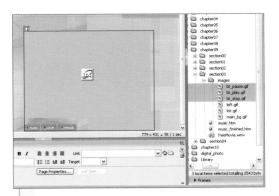

6 From the Files panel, click-and-drag over the Play, Stop, and Pause buttons one at a time and place them below the player. Check that you place the buttons on the layer.

7 Press [F12] to preview your work in the Web browser. So far, ActiveX has only been used to add the music video file to the page and insert the button images. No actions have been given to the button images yet.

8 Select the ActiveX object in the Document window and enter **MediaPlayer1** as the ID in the Properties Inspector. This ID is case-sensitive and must be entered correctly. If you forget to enter the MediaPlayer1 ID in the Properties Inspector, the codes that you will enter in the subsequent steps will not work.

9 Switch to Code View by clicking on the [Show Code View] button (⌨ Code). Enter the JavaScript shown here just below the meta tag to add the OnPlay function. You can see from the script that the OnPlay function is composed of codes on the state of the MediaPlayer1 object.

10 Next, enter the script as shown in step 9 to add the OnStop and OnPause functions. The MediaPlayer1.CurrentPosition=0 code in the OnStop function tells the program to return to the beginning of the movie.

```
<title>music video</title>
<meta http-equiv="Content-Type" content="text/html;
charset=euc-kr'>
    <SCRIPT language=Javascript>
    function OnPlay()
    {
        if (MediaPlayer1.PlayState != 2)
        {
        MediaPlayer1.Play();
        }
    }
    function OnStop()
    {
        MediaPlayer1.Stop();
        MediaPlayer1.CurrentPosition=0;
    }
    function OnPause()
    {
        if (MediaPlayer1.PlayState == 2)
        {
        MediaPlayer1.Pause();
        }
    }
    </SCRIPT>
```

```
<img src="images/bt_play.gif" width="43" height="17">
<img src="images/bt_stop.gif" width="43" height="17">
<img src="images/bt_pause.gif" width="51" height="17">
```

11  Look for the codes for the button images, as shown here.

```
<p>
    <a style="cursor:hand" onClick=OnPlay()><img src="images/bt_play.gif" width="43" height="17"></a>
    <a style="cursor:hand" onClick=OnStop()><img src="images/bt_stop.gif" width="43" height="17"></a>
    <a style="cursor:hand" onClick=OnPause()><img src="images/bt_pause.gif" width="51" height="17"></a>
</p>
```

12  Modify the codes according to what is shown here. Style="cursor:hand" means that when the mouse is over the image, the mouse cursor changes to a hand pointer. OnClick=OnPlay means that when the button is clicked (onClick), the OnPlay function is executed and the movie plays.

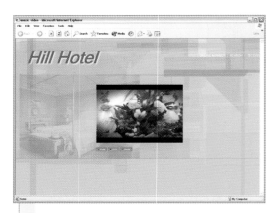

13  Preview your work in the Web browser by pressing [F12]. Since you set up the music video to start automatically (when you entered the parameter AutoStart=1 in step 5), the video will play automatically. Check that the Stop and Pause buttons work properly.

# Using Flash Elements to Make a Slide Show

Dreamweaver MX 2004 includes just one Flash element, the Image Viewer. This feature allows you to insert an SWF file of a slide show into a Web page. You will not need to know Flash in order to use the Image Viewer Flash element in Dreamweaver.

**Start File**
\Sample\Chapter09\Section04\ele.htm

**Final File**
\Sample\Chapter09\Section04\ele_finished.htm

1 First, open ele.htm and select the [Flash elements] category from the Insert bar. Click on the [Image Viewer] icon (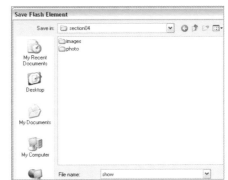). The Image Viewer will let you create Flash files without using Flash.

<< note

### Resource Files

Remember to copy the resource files on the CD-ROM to your local site before you start each exercise in this book.

2 Before proceeding, you need to designate a folder where the SWF file will be saved. In the Save Flash Element dialog box, save the file as **show** in the C:\Sample\Chapter09\Section04\ folder. Click [Save].

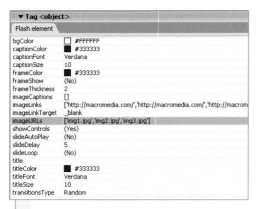

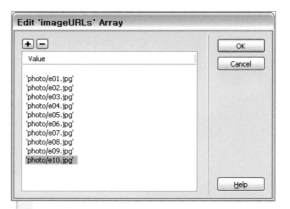

3   The Flash object now appears in the Document window. With the Flash object selected, you will see a variety of different options appear in the Tag Inspector. To select and add the images that will be used in this Flash file, go to imageURLs in the Tag Inspector and click on the [Edit Array Values] icon (⎙).

4   The Edit 'imageURLs' Array dialog box appears. Select the [Add] icon (⊞) to add an image to the list. Click on the [folder] icon (🗀) and select the images from the \Sample\Chapter09 \Section04\photo folder one at a time. Repeat the step for the remaining nine images. After adding all 10 images, click [OK].

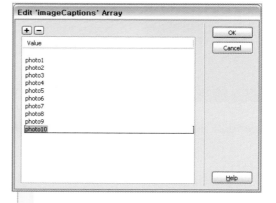

5   Select ImageCaptions in the Tag Inspector and click on Edit Array Values (⎙) to give each image a name.

6   Click on the ⊞ icon to insert an image name. Since you have 10 images, you should have a total of 10 different names. Click [OK].

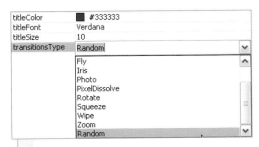

7　Select transitionsType in the Tag Inspector and select an effect for the transition from one image to another. Selecting the Random transition will apply transitions randomly.

8　Click on the [Play] button in the Properties Inspector to preview the Flash movie. You can click on the Next or Previous buttons in the Flash file to switch the images.

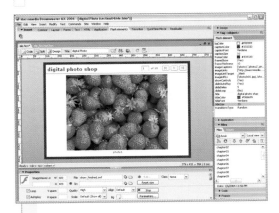

9　In the Tag Inspector, enter the Title as **digital photo shop**, TitleColor as #006699, and TitleSize as 20. In the Properties Inspector, edit the height and width of the Flash file so that W=600 and H=400.

10　In the Tag Inspector, change the frameThickness to 10. Notice that the frameColor is set to #333333. frameThickness is used to set the border thickness and frameColor can be used to change the border color. Units are in pixels. Select Yes for frameShow to display the border.

11　Set slideDelay to 5 and slideAutoPlay to Yes so that a new image will appear every 5 seconds. Preview your work in the Web browser by pressing [F12].

Chapter 10

# Working with Images

With the new Dreamweaver MX 2004, basic image editing can now be done in the program itself. In addition to new image-editing features such as cropping, the new, cross-program integration between Dreamweaver and Fireworks (Macromedia's graphics editor) makes it easier to work with images. In this chapter, you will learn how to use Dreamweaver independently or in conjunction with Fireworks to edit and add images to your Web page.

# Dreamweaver and Fireworks

Although Dreamweaver now contains some image-editing features, it should be remembered that, although it is a powerful Web editor, it is not a graphics editor. Macromedia's Fireworks MX 2004, on the other hand, is a powerful graphics program which you can use to create and edit images, buttons, menus, icons, and more.

## Basic Image Editing in Dreamweaver

In the next section, you will learn to use Fireworks together with Dreamweaver to edit your images. As you will learn in this section, Dreamweaver is suitable for simple image and resolution resizing. However, for more advanced graphics procedures, Fireworks becomes indispensable.

### Resizing Images in Dreamweaver

There are two types of digital images: vector-based and pixel-based images. Vector-based images are described using mathematical equations, while pixel-based images are described using tiny dots called pixels. If you zoom in on an image, you will be able to see the pixels. A pixel-based image is described in terms of the number of pixels along its width and height.

When an image is resized in Dreamweaver, the browser is told to display the image larger or smaller than its actual size. This involves making the pixels larger or smaller. When the pixels become larger, the image will become fuzzier and less sharp. If the pixels become so small that they cannot be shown in the browser, the file size will become unnecessarily large (since the extra data represented by the pixels won't be visible to the user).

1. Open the example file, \Sample\Chapter10\Section00\ex.html. This very large image file (2048×1536 pixels) was taken using a digital camera. Unless you need to show massive images, images this big are not used on Web pages.

2. Click on the (⬚) button in the Image Properties Inspector. Change the width of the image to 600 pixels and the height to 400 pixels.

290

3. You should receive the message shown at the right. Even after you make changes to the image, you can use the undo feature to return the image back to its original state.

4. Load the resized image. This is an easy way to resize images in Dreamweaver without having to use Fireworks.

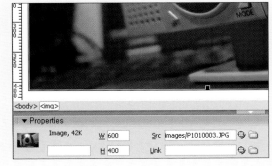

## Cropping Images

Images can also be cropped in Dreamweaver.

1. Selecting the image, click on the [Crop] button ( ) in the Image Properties Inspector.

2. Select the desired area in the picture.

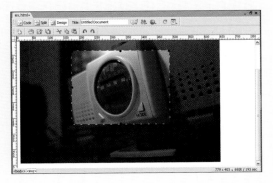

3. Click on the [Crop] button (⬚) again to crop the image.

## Adjusting Brightness and Contrast

Select the image and click on the [Brightness and Contrast] button (◑) in the Properties Inspector.

In the Brightness/Contrast dialog box, adjust the image's brightness and contrast using the slider bars, or by typing in the values directly.

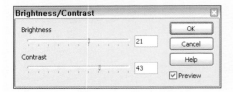

## Sharpening Images in Dreamweaver

Select the image and then click on the [Sharpen] button (△) to sharpen the image.

## Using Dreamweaver Together with Fireworks

Because Dreamweaver and Fireworks are both developed by Macromedia, they are 100% compatible and Fireworks functions have been integrated with Dreamweaver. For example, the Image Properties Inspector in Dreamweaver MX 2004 has the same menu as that used in Fireworks. Of course, in order to use this menu, you must have Fireworks MX 2004 installed on your computer.

## Resizing Images in Fireworks

Here, the simple process of opening a large file in Fireworks for resizing will be used to demonstrate the compatibility of Dreamweaver and Fireworks.

1. To work with the image, click on it, go to the Image Properties Inspector, and click the [Edit] icon (🖉). Clicking the icon will launch Fireworks MX 2004.

2. You will be asked if you wish to use the PNG file format (a file format exclusive to Fireworks). If the image was created in Fireworks, click on [Use a PNG] and locate the source file. Otherwise click on [Use This File], which will allow you to edit the JPG file directly. In this example, click Use This File .

3. Click on an empty space on the screen so that the image is no longer selected and select [Modify] - [Canvas] - [Image Size].

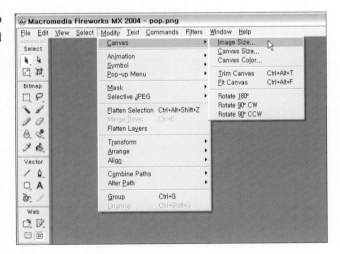

4. Enter 600 pixels by 450 pixels for the image size and click [OK].

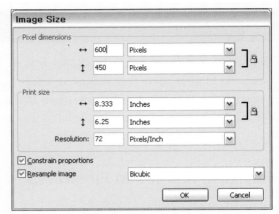

<< tip

## Set Magnification to 100%

The [Magnifying Glass] button (🔍) in Fireworks can be used to adjust the view, and it is a good idea to get in the habit of viewing images at 100%. If the view is set to, say 50%, it is easy to forget this is not the true image size, and you will get incorrect results when you import it to Dreamweaver.

5. After resizing the image, click the [Done] button (Done) at the top of the Document window and go back to Dreamweaver.

6. When you go back to Dreamweaver, you will see in the Properties Inspector that the size of the image hasn't changed but the W and H values are in boldface. The boldface is an indication that this is not the current size of the image, which has been altered. Click on the [Refresh] button (🔄) to update the size information.

294

7. When you refresh the size data, the image will change to the size that you designated in Fireworks. As you can see in the Properties Inspector here, the image file size is currently 47k, down from the original 692k.

## Optimizing Images

Optimizing an image in this case means making the image's file size smaller. Through a reduction in quality you can keep the image dimensions but make a smaller file that will speed up the page loading time.

1. Selecting the image, go to the Image Properties Inspector in Dreamweaver and click on the [Optimize in Fireworks] button ( ). This will give you all the information about the current image in Fireworks.

2. Set the image quality to 70%. Now look at your image. If there is no visible difference in the image, you can safely lower the image quality some more. Selecting the image quality is entirely up to you and your own personal preference. For the sake of this exercise, an image quality of 70% will work fine. When you're done, click [ Update ].

3. If you look at the image file size again, you can see that it has been reduced from 47k to 24k.

# Slicing Images

When working on Web pages, you often need to cut images to fit them into the cells of a table. This is tedious and time consuming. In Fireworks and other graphics programs, you will find the Slice tool, which makes the job easier. In Fireworks, not only can you slice images, you can also save them directly as HTML documents and save them to the Dreamweaver library.

**Start File**

\Sample\Chapter10\Section01\main\pop.png

**Final File**

\Sample\Chapter10\Section01\slice_finished.html

<< note

### Resource Files

Remember to copy the resource files on the CD-ROM to your local site before you start each exercise in this book.

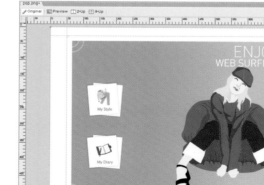

1  Start Fireworks MX 2004 and open the pop.png file. Show the rulers by selecting [View] - [Rulers] or by hitting [Ctrl]-[Alt]-[r]. Click on the horizontal ruler and, without releasing the mouse, drag towards the image so that a green guideline appears as shown. Repeat this step for the vertical ruler.

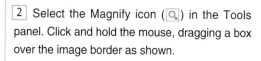

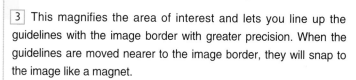

2 Select the Magnify icon (🔍) in the Tools panel. Click and hold the mouse, dragging a box over the image border as shown.

3 This magnifies the area of interest and lets you line up the guidelines with the image border with greater precision. When the guidelines are moved nearer to the image border, they will snap to the image like a magnet.

4 Drag out more guidelines over the image. These guidelines will mark out the area you wish to slice, as shown here.

5 Select the Slice tool (📝) from the Tools panel. Click and drag out green boxes as shown. The green boxes are the areas that will be used.

<< note
### Shortcut Key

If you are using another tool and want to move the guidelines, hold down the [Ctrl] key and your current tool cursor will change into an arrow pointer. Without releasing the [Ctrl] key, move the arrow pointer near the guidelines and it will turn into a double-headed arrow pointer. This indicates that you can move the guidelines.

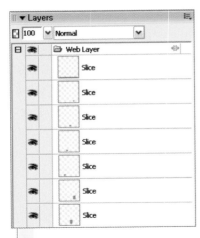

6 In the Layers panel, you will see that a new layer is added for every green area. The layers in Fireworks are slightly different from the Dreamweaver layers you are familiar with. In Dreamweaver, you have to draw out a layer and decide on the location and size of the layer on the Web page. But in Fireworks, layers are automatically created in the size of the canvas, and they cover the canvas exactly.

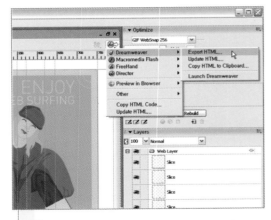

7 Once you are done, save your work as a Dreamweaver HTML file by clicking on the Quick Export icon (), then selecting [Dream weaver] - [Export HTML].

8 Select your destination folder and name the file **main.htm**, then click [Save]. The image will be sliced and the HTML document created automatically.

298

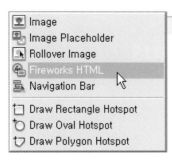

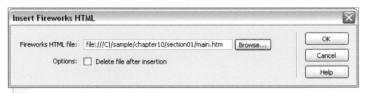

9  Although you can open the Fireworks HTML file directly in Dreamweaver, it is recommended that you first create a new file (**slice.htm**) in Dreamweaver and then import the HTML file main.html. Start Dreamweaver and create a new file, **slice.htm**. Then from the Insert bar, select the [Common] category, click on the [Images] icon ( 🖼 ), and select [Fireworks HTML].

10  Click the [Browse] button, locate the main.html file, and click [OK] when done.

11  The HTML file you created in Fireworks will be inserted as a table in Dreamweaver. The slices indicate table cells.

12  Looking at the Src text field at the bottom of the Properties Inspector, you will see the path of the original Fireworks file, pop.png. If you click the [Edit] button ( 🖼 Edit ), you can make further changes to your original file in Fireworks. To view the path of the file, you must check that the Fireworks table is selected.

# Making Pop-Up Menus in Fireworks

In Chapter 7, you learned to create a pop-up menu in Dreamweaver. In this exercise, you will learn to do this in Fireworks. Although you will find many of the steps here identical to the exercise on making the pop-up menu in Dreamweaver, there are some differences. Using Fireworks, you can set the area that responds to the mouse-over event with more flexibility. You can also position the pop-up menu by dragging it in the Document window.

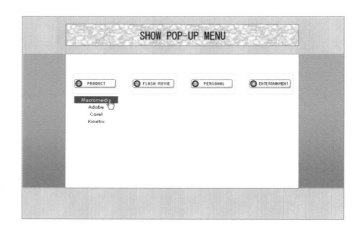

**Start File**

\Sample\Chapter10\Section02\pop-up.png

**Final File**

\Sample\Chapter10\Section02\pop-up_finished.htm

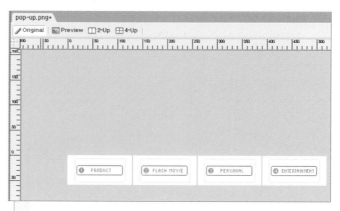

1 Launch Fireworks and open pop-up.png. You will see that this file contains four menu images.

2  Use the Slice tool () to create four slices; one for each menu image. Be precise when drawing the four slices.

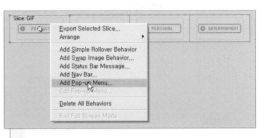

3  Right-click on the Product slice and select [Add Pop-up Menu].

4  In the Pop-up Menu Editor dialog box, check that the [Contents] tab is selected. Enter **Macromedia** in the text field, enter **http://www. macromedia.com** in the Link field, and choose _blank from the Target options.

5  Next, let's add new items to the list. Enter the text shown here in the Text and Link fields. For all the items, select the _blank option in the Target field. What you've done here is to add the sub-menus that will pop up when the Product menu is moused over. Click [Next] when you are done.

| Text | Link |
|------|------|
| Adobe | http://www.adobe.com |
| Corel | http://www.corel.com |
| Kinetix | http://www.ktx.com |

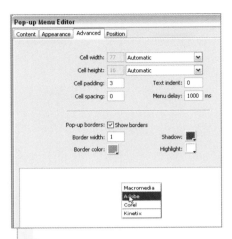

6 When the Appearance category appears, select the Vertical menu option. Select the [Verdana, Arial, Helvetica, sans-serif] font option, set font size to 10, alignment to center, and the Over State Cell Color to Maroon. A preview of the sub-menu is shown at the bottom of the dialog box. Click [Next].

7 In the Advanced category, you can decide on more advanced appearance settings. One thing to note here is that the 1000 ms in Menu Delay refers to 1 second. This means that the pop-up menu will remain visible for one second after the mouse is taken off the image. You may leave the default settings alone or experiment with the options. Click [Next].

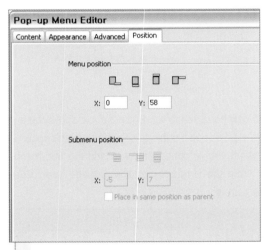

8 In the Position category, click on the [Set Menu Position to Bottom of Slice] button (▣). Next, click [Done].

9 In the Document window, you will see an outline of the pop-up menu. In Fireworks, you can select and move the pop-up menu around. You won't be able do this if you are creating the pop-up menu in Dreamweaver.

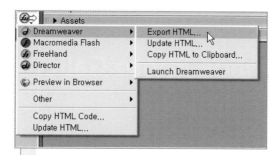

**10** Click on the [Quick Export] icon and select [Dreamweaver] - [Export HTML].

**11** Click on the [Advanced] tab where you can decide on more advanced appearance settings. One thing to note here is that the 1000 ms in Menu Delay refers to 1 second. This means that the pop-up menu will remain visible for one second after the mouse is taken off the image. You may leave the default settings alone or experiment with the options.

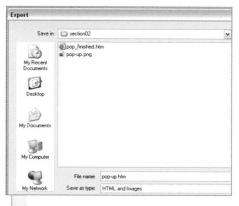

**12** In the Export dialog box, enter the **pop-up.htm** file name, select a folder to save in, and click [Save].

**13** To use the pop-up menu in Dreamweaver, launch Dreamweaver and create a new Web page. In the Insert bar, select the [Common] category, click on the [Image] button ( ) and select [Fireworks HTML].

**14** In the Insert Fireworks HTML dialog box, browse for the pop up.htm file. Click [OK].

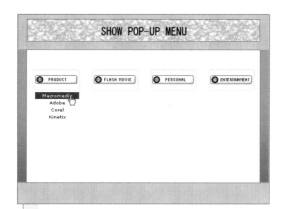

**15** Hit [F12] for a preview in the Web browser. Mouse over the menu to check if the sub-menu pops up.

**16** When you click on an option on the pop-up menu, a new browser window will open and the corresponding Web site will load. Note that everything works and appears just as you made it in Fireworks.

# Creating an Online Photo Gallery

With the increasing popularity of digital cameras, more people are taking digital pictures and putting them on the Web. In this exercise, you will find creating web photo albums a breeze and, through the process, realize how truly seamless the integration of Fireworks and Dreamweaver is.

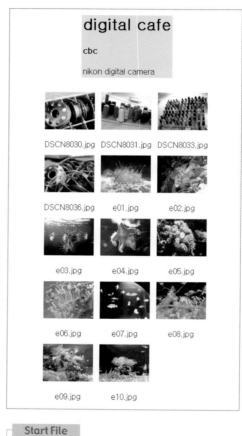

**Start File**

\Sample\digital_photo\

**Final File**

\Sample\digital_photo\resize\index.htm

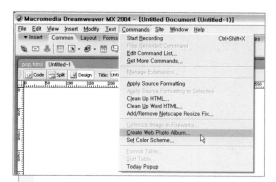

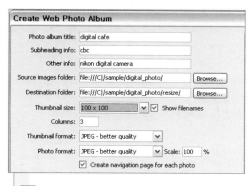

**1** In Dreamweaver, create a new document. From the main menu, select [Commands] - [Create Web Photo Album].

**2** In the Create Web Photo Album dialog box, enter **digital cafe** as the photo album title, **cbc** as the Subheading info, and **nikon digital camera** as the other info. Browse to /Sample/digital_photo for the source images folder, and /Sample/digital_photo/resize for the destination folder. Set thumbnail size to 100 X 100 and columns to 3. Choose [JPEG - better quality] in the Thumbnail format and Photo format options. Set scale to 100%. Check the [Show filenames] and [Create navigation page for each photo] options. Click [OK].

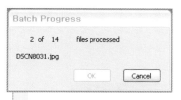

**3** Fireworks MX will start up automatically to process the images. In the Batch Progress dialog box, you can see how many images have been processed and how many there are in total.

**4** When the dialog box indicates the album has been created, click [OK].

**5** You will be sent to the Dreamweaver interface. You will see that the index.htm document has been created automatically.

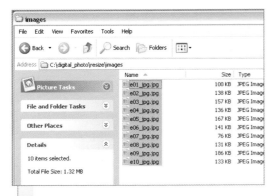

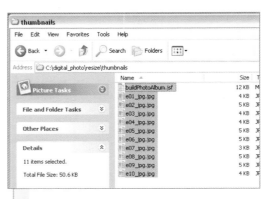

6 Go to Windows Explorer and look for the /Sample/digital_photo folder which you set as the source images folder. As expected, you will find all the images in the folder.

7 Open the resize folder that you set as the destination folder earlier. You will find that the images, pages, and thumbnails folders –as well as the index.htm document–have been created. The images folder contains duplicates of the original images. When you resize the images (as you did in step 1), the altered image will be saved in the images folder.

8 Double-click on the index.htm document to see the photo album in the Web browser.

9 When you click on a thumbnail, a new Web page containing the original image and the Previous, Home, and Next links will appear in the same browser window. While processing in Fireworks, a new HTML page for every thumbnail image was created automatically. And because you checked the [Create navigation page for each photo] option, the links will appear at the top of the page.

# Index › › ›